W9-APG-483

The generations that fashioned these romances are not merely our spiritual ancestors, but to some extent our physical as well. They are inside our bones—unknown to us; and when we listen, they are listening too. As we read, some dim ancestral ego of which we are unaware may be nodding approvingly on hearing again its own old tale, rejoicing to recognize again what once was a part of its own old wisdom.

—HEINRICH ZIMMER

MYTHS AND MODERN MAN

BARBARA STANFORD
with Gene Stanford

Designed and Illustrated
by Jay and Sherwood Roper

Washington Square Press
Pocket Books • New York

MYTHS AND MODERN MAN

WASHINGTON SQUARE PRESS edition published December, 1972

Published by
POCKET BOOKS, a division of Simon & Schuster, Inc.
630 Fifth Avenue, New York, N.Y. 10020.

WASHINGTON SQUARE PRESS editions are distributed
in the U.S. by Simon & Schuster, Inc., 630 Fifth Avenue,
New York, N.Y. 10020 and in Canada by Simon & Schuster of Canada, Ltd., Richmond Hill, Ontario, Canada.

For Jewel Richie and Marie Smith

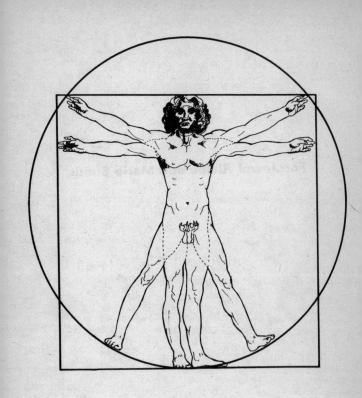

man the myth maker

Man is always asking questions.
He begins as soon as he is able to talk:
Mommy, where did I come from?
What makes the lightning?
Why do dogs have four legs?
What will happen to me after I die?

And he continues asking throughout his life
No matter how sophisticated he may become:
Whom should I marry?
Why are people turning to drugs?
Can we cure cancer?
What is on the moon—on Mars—on . . . ?

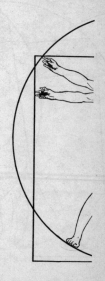

Often there are no answers
Or the answers cannot be expressed in
  simple terms
Or they are hard to understand.
And so the answers are told in stories:

Once upon a time little Red Riding Hood . . .
In the early days, the coyote . . .
A certain man went down from Jericho to
  Jerusalem . . .
Imagine a ball with nine smaller balls going
  around it . . .

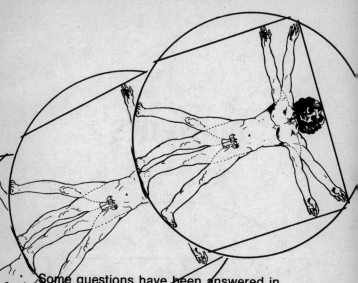

Some questions have been answered in scientific terms.
But the most important questions can still only be answered by stories
That express the deepest wisdom and insight
That the human race has accumulated over thousands of years.
These are the myths.
And the questions they answer
Connect the most primitive cave dwellers
And the most sophisticated apartment dwellers:
Where did we come from?
How do men and women differ?
What is the perfect man?
Can men live together in peace?
Is death the end?

contents

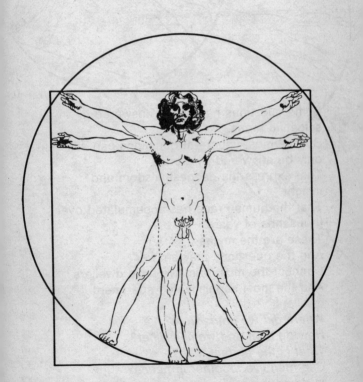

nning in the
g in the beg
nning in the
eginning in
ng in the be
e beginnin

Where Did We Come From?

How Do Men and Women Differ?

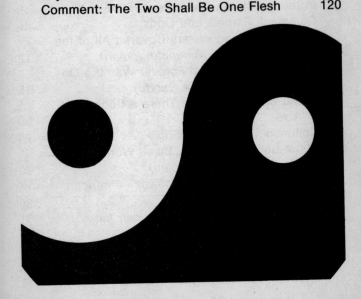

What Is the Perfect Man?

Can Men Live Together in Peace?

death

Is Death the End?

WHERE DID WE COME FROM?

in the beginning in the
beginning in the
beginning in the
beginning in the bec

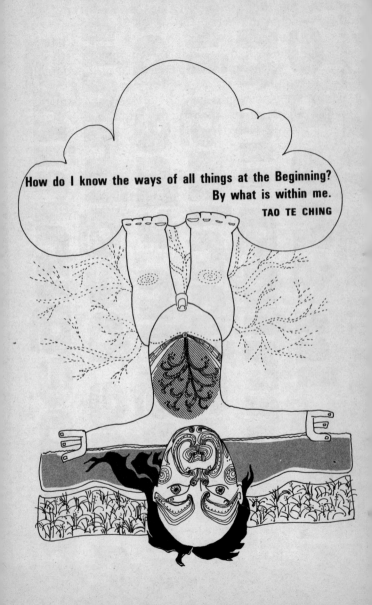

How do I know the ways of all things at the Beginning?
By what is within me.

TAO TE CHING

there was nothing

And from nothing came darkness, and then light, and finally the sky and the earth. And Rangi, the sky, and Papa, the earth, came together in love and had many children.

But Rangi and Papa were joined inseparably, so that their children had no place to live but were squeezed into the tight darkness between them. At last their offspring crept together to confer about their fate. Tu, the god of man and war, said, "Let's kill Rangi and Papa so we'll be freed."

But Tane, the god of the forest, said, "No, let's try to separate them. Maybe we won't have to kill them. If we try hard enough, we can push the sky away and keep Mother Earth to nurse us."

So first Rongo, god of cultivated food, tried to force the heaven and earth apart. But he failed. Then Tangaroa, god of all the animals that live in the sea, tried, but he too had no luck. Then Haumia, father of wild plants, also tried and failed. Warlike Tu then took his knife and hacked away the sinews that bound earth and heaven, but he still could not separate them.

At last, Tane, god of the trees, placed his shoulders against the earth and his feet against the sky and pressed with all of his might. He thrust the sky above him and held him there.

Now at last all of the children of Rangi and Papa could stand up and see the light.

Since there was room upon the earth, Tane decided to make some people. He went to the spot where Rangi's blood had fallen when Tu chopped on him and picked up some of the clay. Tane was a god, but he had a man's interest, so he made a woman. Soon she had a beautiful daughter whom he named Hine Titama.

When Hine Titama grew up she was very beautiful, so Tane also married her and she bore him several children. But she did not know that Tane was her father.

One day she asked Tane, "Who is my father?"

For a long time Tane did not answer. At last he told her the truth.

Hine Titama cried out in horror, "How could you make me commit such a dreadful crime! I can't bear to live with this shame!"

So Hine Titama ran sorrowfully to her grandmother Papa in the deep, dark center of the earth. There she was comforted. And since that time all of mankind has followed her on the trail of death.

When the world was created ..... upon Asase Ya, mother Earth. But not all respectful of Wulbari. that men could reach up right into Wulbari's eyes. They would were dirty, they would reach up piece off of him and wipe them off on Wulbari. One old woman would cut a and put it into her soup every day. At last Wulbari became so annoyed at the way he was treated by men that he moved up higher into the sky.

so close were Wulbari who was God lay men But would blow over the fires and smoke their hands food Wulbari as a towel. Whenever they

were ice and fire

And the two came together and formed a mist. And from these mists, Ymir, the frost giant, was formed. Next, the mist formed a great cow who fed Ymir. The cow gained her nourishment by eating the ice and frost, but one day as she was eating, a hair appeared. As she continued eating, she uncovered the whole head of some new being. At last she kicked free the whole body of the god Bori.

Ymir, in the meantime, continued to grow from the cow's milk and had a number of children from the mist. One of his daughters married Bori, and they had sons and grandsons. His grandsons Odin, Vili, and Ve decided that Ymir, the frost giant, was evil and that they should kill him.

From the dead frost giant's body the new gods made the earth. From his blood they made the seas. They built the mountains out of his bones and the trees out of his hair.

From the body of Ymir grew a mighty ash tree, Yggdrasil, which supports the whole universe. This tree has three immense roots: the first goes to Midgard, the land of man; the second goes to Jotunheim, the land of the giants; and the third to Niflheim, the region of death. The root to Midgard is carefully guarded by the Norns, or fates.

The gods built themselves a home called Asgard which can be reached only by crossing the rainbow, Bilfrost. There Odin lives with his wife, Frigga, and sons Thor, Vithar, Bragi, Balder, and Hoder.

THURSDAY					
{ from Thor, Norse God of the Sky					

WEDNESDAY					
{ From Odin, known also as Woden, Chief Norse God					

4

was chaos

Night, mist, and ether whirled in confusion until at last they formed themselves into an egg. Gathering speed, the whirling chaos suddenly split in two, forming Father Heaven (Uranus) and Mother Earth (Gaea). And between them floated Eros, or Love.

As Love touched him, Uranus showered a fertile rain on Gaea and from her womb sprang mountains, woods, and meadows. Then came living creatures: hundred-handed monsters, one-eyed Cyclops, and gigantic Titans. Uranus was horrified at the sight of the hundred-handed monsters and banished them to a deep pit called Tartarus.

Gaea was insulted by this treatment that her children were given, for she loved them all even if they were ugly, so she plotted with her youngest son, Cronus, to kill Uranus. That night the son waited for his father with a sickle and when Uranus came by, Cronus leaped out and slashed the old god to bits. The blood of the great sky god fell upon the sea and was washed up on the shore of Cythera in ocean foam. And from this blood sprang the beautiful goddess of love and beauty, Aphrodite.

But Cronus was an even worse ruler than his father, Uranus. To begin with, he did not free his hundred-handed monster brothers, whose imprisonment was supposedly the reason he had killed his father. Gaea was so angry at Cronus that she vowed that one of his own children would dethrone him, just as he had dethroned his father.

Cronus thought he was too smart for her. He went ahead and married his sister Rhea and waited for the children to come along. As soon

5

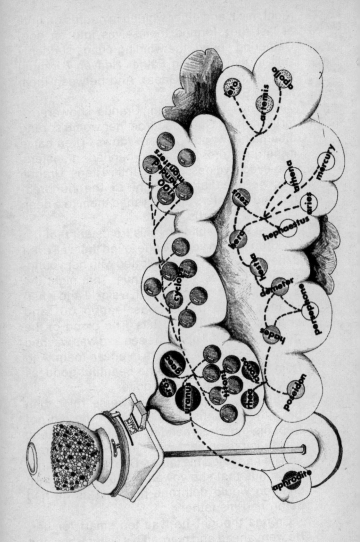

6

as they were born, he swallowed them so they would not be able to dethrone him. Five children—Hestia, Demeter, Hera, Poseidon, and Hades—were born and immediately swallowed by their father. But Rhea did not like this treatment of her children any better than Gaea had appreciated the imprisonment of her monsters.

So when she became pregnant with her sixth child, Rhea decided that she would trick her husband. When it was time for the baby to be born, she slipped off to a cave in Crete and left the infant there in charge of a gentle nymph. Then she returned to Cronus with a large stone wrapped in swaddling clothes. Cronus did not bother to unwrap the bundle, but swallowed it whole, not noticing that the taste and texture were somewhat different from his first five children.

So, Zeus, the youngest child of Cronus, lived and grew to manhood. His grandmother, Gaea, who had prompted Cronus to kill Uranus, was now more than eager to have Cronus overthrown, so she gave the young god an herb which would make Cronus vomit. Zeus managed to slip it into his food, and Cronus went into a vomiting fit. First the stone came up, and then the five brothers and sisters, who were—amazingly—still alive. The six children placed the stone at Delphi, where it stands today, and fled away to begin plotting their father's downfall.

Thus began the great battle of the gods. Cronus and all his Titan brothers, with their gigantic strength, were arrayed against the young gods. But Gaea was still trying to rescue her monster children from Tartarus and offered their services to Zeus if he would let them loose. So Zeus flew to Tartarus and let loose the Cyclops and the hundred-handed monsters, and with their help he conquered the Titans. The Cyclops were so grateful at being freed that they made the thunderbolt and lightning. They gave Poseidon a magic trident which could cause the earth to shake, and they gave Hades a magic helmet which made him invisible.

Zeus and his two brothers divided the control of the world, with Zeus receiving the heavens and earth, Poseidon the sea, and Hades the underworld. Zeus and his family made their homes on Mount Olympus, where they feasted on ambrosia and watched the affairs of men.

Zeus married his sister Hera, who was also known as Juno, but he was never very faithful. In fact, most of the heroes of Greece could trace their ancestry to Zeus and one of his human lovers, whom he usually visited in the form of an animal such as a swan or a bull. Hera was very jealous of Zeus and did her best to bring his human lovers and children to a sad end.

Zeus also had affairs with other goddesses, particularly the goddess Leto. Hera fiercely attacked Leto and drove her from land to land. Pregnant with twins, Leto fled from country to country until she came to a desolate floating island called Delos and there at last delivered her daughter, Artemis. A rather precocious child, Artemis assisted at the birth of her twin brother, Apollo, a few hours later.

Apollo was the god of light, music, and masculine beauty. He made known the will of the gods, gave judgments, and offered purification from sin through his oracle at Delphi, where he inspired the priestess to speak his message.

His sister Artemis was a virgin huntress, protectress of wild things, and goddess of the moon. As Greek culture spread, she took on

the names and characteristics of other goddesses of the moon, so she is variously known
as Cynthia, Selena, Hecate, and Diana, and her
character varied from the chaste, shy goddess
of the wood who killed a man who saw her
naked, to the multi-breasted fertility goddess
of Ephesus.

Hermes, or Mercury, was another of Zeus'
rather precocious offspring. On the day of his
birth he invented the lyre and stole Apollo's
cattle. However, the clever trickster made
friends with his brother by giving him the lyre,
and Apollo was so enraptured with the beautiful
music of this instrument that he forgot all about
punishing Hermes for stealing his cattle.
Hermes became the chief messenger of the
gods and the conductor of dead souls to
Hades, the land of the dead.

Athena's birth was the most unusual of all
the Olympian gods; for she sprang fully grown
and in complete armor from Zeus' head. Always
one of Zeus' favorites, she was allowed to carry
his breastplate. Athena represented wisdom,
justice, and law, and was associated with the
city of Athens, which she won in a contest with
Poseidon. She greatly admired courage and
frequently assisted heroes in their exploits.

Strangely, the children of Zeus' legitimate
wife, Hera, were among the less attractive of
the gods. Hephaestus, or Vulcan, was born
lame, and Hera was so upset that she threw
the child from Mount Olympus. Only when he
became powerful by learning to shape iron and
bronze did the gods invite him back.

Their other child, Ares or Mars, was the god
of war. Unlike the other gods, who were willing
to fight only when they needed to, Ares simply
enjoyed the blood and gore—at least as long
as it was from others. When he joined in the

Trojan War, he was quickly wounded and came scampering back whimpering to his disgusted father.

So the Greek universe was peopled with gods and goddesses representing many different aspects of the world but behaving in very human fashion. Two dynasties of gods have been overthrown since the world emerged from chaos, and Zeus himself may someday be overthrown, perhaps by man.

Geography (from Gaea, Greek goddess of the earth): the study of the earth

Aphrodisiac (from Aphrodite, Greek goddess of love and beauty): a substance that increases sexual desire

Hades (from Hades, the Greek underworld): hell

Uranium (from Uranus, Greek god of the sky): a radioactive metallic element

Nuptial (from nymph, Greek divine maiden): relating to marriage

Titanic (from Titans, giants in Greek mythology): of great size or power

June (from Juno, Roman equivalent of Hera, Greek goddess of marriage): sixth month

Mercury (from Mercury, Roman equivalent of Hermes, Greek messenger god): a heavy metallic element that is liquid at ordinary temperatures

Vulcanize (from Vulcan, Roman equivalent of Hephaestus, Greek god of fire and metalwork): to treat synthetic rubber chemically to give it special properties such as strength and elasticity

Martial (from Mars, Roman equivalent of Ares, Greek god of war): relating to war

Erotic (from Eros, Greek god of love): arousing sexual love or desire

PLANETS AND GODS

Mercury, Venus, Earth, Mars, Jupiter, Saturn, Uranus, Neptune, Pluto. It was not just the whim of some medieval scholar which caused the planets of our solar system and the constellations of our sky to be named for mythological figures. Almost every mythological system had gods of the sun and the moon, and most of these included planets and constellations named for various gods. These names were frequently associated with a belief in astrology, and the signs of the zodiac appear with slightly different names in the mythologies of Greece, the Mid-East, India, and China.

Mercury, the messenger god, became associated with the fast-moving first planet of the solar system and also with the slippery metal, quicksilver. Both the Babylonians and the Greeks gave the bright and beautiful evening star the name of their goddess of love. The red color of the planet Mars was observed by the astronomers of the Babylonians and Sumerians, and was therefore given the name of the god of war. Jupiter, the largest planet, was given the name of the chief god.

The qualities associated with the planet Saturn are a result of a confusion between the Roman Saturn and the Greek Cronus, whose only real connection was being the father of the head god, Jupiter and Zeus, respectively. The Roman Saturn was a lively, jovial agricultural god whose long festival, the Saturnalia, was a time when society was turned upside down and slaves were treated like masters. The characteristics associated with Saturn by astrologers are those of the old Greek Cronus, who bequeathed the ideas of death, misery, and gloom to the planet with the Roman name.

Uranus, Neptune, and Pluto were not known by the ancients, but modern astronomers followed their tradition and named these planets after other Roman gods when they discovered them.

waters covered all of the earth

On the surface of the waters were the giant rabbit and the other animals on a raft.

The animals were tired of living on the raft and wanted to find land. So the giant rabbit told the beaver to dive down for land. But the beaver dived as deep as he could and found nothing. Next the giant rabbit sent the otter, but he too returned, exhausted, with no sign of land.

Finally the female muskrat offered to dive. The other animals laughed at her, but the giant rabbit gave her permission to try. She was gone for a whole day and a whole night, and the animals gave her up for lost. Finally, though, they saw her floating on the surface, belly up. The giant rabbit quickly hauled her aboard. He examined her claws and finally found a speck of mud. She had been successful.

The giant rabbit needed only one speck of mud. He worked with it until he made it into mountains, continents, and—finally—the whole world.

and forever was the one, the absolute, iswara

HINDU

The whole world, everything that exists, comes from the One, the Absolute, the Universal Spirit, or Iswara. The Universal Spirit is manifested in three forms: Brahma, the creator, Vishnu, the preserver, and Siva, the destroyer. The world itself exists and disappears as Brahma sleeps and wakes up. Each time Brahma awakens, the world of physical beings appears. When he goes to sleep, the world is absorbed into the Universal Spirit. A day in Brahma's life is equal to 43,200,000 years on earth. Eventually, after 100 years of Brahma's life, the entire universe, including Brahma himself, will be absorbed into Iswara and remain for 100 years.

The world between cycles of creation is sometimes pictured as Vishnu lying motionless on a thousand-headed cobra called Ananta, or eternity, floating on an infinite and unmoving ocean of milk. Then from Vishnu's navel a lotus emerges with Brahma seated on it. Before beginning the work of creation, Brahma submits to a number of austerities to build up his spiritual power. Then he begins by creating opposites—gods and demons.

Another way of visualizing the beginning of creation in the Hindu tradition is as a golden, cosmic egg floating on the waters. At the beginning of the cycle of creation, the egg breaks open to reveal Purusha, a manifestation of the Ultimate Being with a thousand thighs, a thou-

15

sand eyes, a thousand faces, and a thousand heads. Purusha offers himself as a sacrifice for the creation of the universe, and from each of his limbs an object of creation appears. From his mouth issue the Brahmans and the gods. From his abdomen come demons. From his thighs come the merchant caste and cattle. Manual workers and horses come from his feet. In this picturesque way, the myth emphasizes that all of creation has come from the One and will return to it.

Vishnu is most closely involved in human affairs, for frequently his work requires that he come to earth in human form to save the world from premature destruction. Usually his task is to kill a demon who has gained tremendous spiritual powers through meditation and threatens to overpower the gods.

At times Vishnu appears as an animal. One appearance was as a fish when the great flood came. He appeared to the great sage Manu as a fish, warned Manu to build a boat, and floated near him so that Manu could anchor his boat to him.

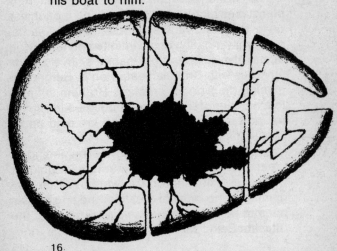

In another story of the flood, the earth was held under the waters by a demon. Vishnu took the form of a boar and dived deep into the depths, where he killed the demon and raised the earth back to its proper place.

Other appearances were as a lion, as a dwarf who had the power to grow to gigantic size, and as two important heroes, Rama and ·Krishna.

The final appearance of Vishnu is yet to come. He will appear riding on a white horse and will bring in the end of the age—and the work of Siva.

Siva, the third of the trinity, is the god of destruction—the destruction of the old, worn-out world. He prepares the way for all to be reabsorbed into the Eternal One and for the re-creation of the world. Siva is also associated with asceticism—the destruction of evil in the human being so that the individual soul may be reabsorbed into the One and be freed from the world of illusion.

17

As the life of man has its season, so does the life of the universe. The universe is observed to be expanding at a prodigious rate. The galaxies and dust clouds of which it is made are receding from one another at speeds up to that of light. A gigantic explosion is in progress. Some eleven billion years ago the universe was supposedly confined to a tiny space, formless, but possessing great potency, great energy. In an instant, the fundamental physical constraints, like the charge on the electron, were decided by chance; then the physical laws of our universe took over and there was a tremendous explosion—the "big bang." Eventually the energy of the explosion will be used up, and the expansion will slow to a halt because of the gravitational attraction of all the pieces of matter for one another. The universe will thereupon contract, ultimately down to the same exceedingly tiny space in which it was born. The scenario will then repeat, with different fundamental constants. There will be a cyclic creation and destruction of universes, all subtly different. Each cycle is believed to take about eighty billion years, so there is no need to panic.

JOHN W. CLARK

"At eighteen, I thought that the theory presented in our astronomy class was the 'truth' and that my friend's belief, the Biblical one, was mere fantasy. It should have given me pause, however, that the theory propounded in college was not the one I had learned in high school, only three or four years earlier. My high school teacher told us about the Laplace nebular hypothesis to account for the origin of the earth and the solar system; whereas now, in college, I was being given the Chamberlin-Moulton planetesimal hypothesis."

—Philip Freund

In the beginning —was there a beginning?

No one knows. Man only knows that this earth has been created and destroyed many many times. And it will be destroyed again.

The last time the world was destroyed and re-created, there were no men on it. Quetzalcoatl, the plumed serpent god, saw that the earth was empty. So he went to the world of the dead and collected the bones of the dead people of the past. He gathered the bones together, but they did not live because they had no blood. So Quetzalcoatl cut himself and gave mankind his own blood so that they might live.

Since the god's blood was shed for man, man must continue to shed his blood so the gods can continue to live. Human beings must be sacrificed regularly or the sun and the earth will die.

Creation, in many mythologies, appears to be a bloody, painful process. Ymir and Purusha were dismembered and all living things were made from their broken bodies. Quetzalcoatl gave his own blood for life, and Papa and Rangi were violently torn apart. And in mythologies and religions in which creation itself is not painful, sacrifice often appears as a necessary part of the redemption or further evolution of the creation.

Furthermore, sacrifice is almost universal in the rituals needed to appease the gods and to assure the continuation of the world. The Aztecs believed that they were forced to kill a large number of human beings each day to feed the sun and keep it in the sky. Greeks sacrificed bulls; Africans, cocks; Hebrews, lambs; and Incas, llamas, to their various gods and spirits.

Self-mutilation was another common form of sacrifice in most of the world. The Norse god Odin sacrificed one of his eyes to attain knowledge, and in Australia, Africa, and the Middle East, young men endured circumcision to attain their position as men in their society. Ritual enduring of pain was a part of the American Plains Indian Sun Dance, yoga exercises in Asia, and Christian penitential ceremonies.

In the Plains Indian Sun Dance, the pain was associated with the renewal of the earth, as it was to some extent in almost every culture. Man's birth is painful, his weaning is painful, and almost every step of emotional and social growth is accompanied by the pain of separation from old friends and old ways of life. Man only lives by daily sacrificing the lives of plants or animals that are weaker than he. So it is not illogical that the earth too was born in pain, lives through the sacrifices of others, and will die in pain.

21

I think that a study of myths for their own sake would be an idle affair, a species of dilettantism, for which I have neither the time nor the temperament. What held my interest, almost from the very start, was the hint that I might learn something fundamental and permanent about the mind of man—about myself—by contemplating mythology, and especially man's always daring stories of "the beginning."

MYTHS OF CREATION BY PHILIP FREUND
WASHINGTON SQUARE PRESS, INC. NEW YORK. 1965

In the beginning was a black world of fire

The first world was inhabited by insects and insectlike people. It was such an unpleasant place that all of the insects made themselves wings and flew to the sky to look for a new home. Finally they found a crack in the sky and emerged into the second world.

The second world was a blue world of birds who strongly resented the invasion of the insect people. There was constant fighting, and at last the insect people followed the voice of the blue wind to the third world.

The third world, or yellow world, began to look more like the world we now know, and people and animals began to look more like they do now. There were four mountains in this land, one in each direction, and the mountain people began to teach First Man and First Woman how to plant corn and how to build homes. They also warned everyone not to bother the water monster.

But the coyote did not heed the warnings. He went to the home of the water monster and kidnapped his two children.

Suddenly the oceans rose and the land began to flood. All of the people and animals gathered on top of the highest mountain. The people planted a giant reed on top of the mountain and climbed up inside it. Finally after four days of climbing the giant reed, they reached the fourth world.

This fourth world was even more beautiful than those before, and here were other people

23

and other kinds of animals. Here First Man and First Woman learned more about growing corn and the proper roles for the sexes.

But the coyote still had the children of the water monster, and First People were horrified to find the waters of their new world suddenly rising. Again they planted a reed and began to climb, but this time they could not reach all the way. Nor could they find a hole. So the yellow hawk tried to scratch a hole in the dome. The heron and the buzzard also helped, but the locust was the one who finally succeeded in getting through. Then the spider spun a rope so that everyone could climb up through the hole.

The new world was only a small island, so the ants went first, carrying the soil of the fourth world. The other people followed, carrying seeds of corn and other treasures from the fourth world.

The people had not even gotten settled in the fifth world when the waters there started rising. This time First Man and First Woman decided that someone must have offended the water monster. They searched everyone, and of course, found his children with the coyote. They took them to the lake and put them in a small boat. The waters went down immediately and floods have never again destroyed man's world.

WHAT IS MAN?

When I consider thy heavens,
The work of thy fingers
The moon and the stars,
Which Thou hast ordained.

What is man that Thou art mindful of him?
And the son of man that Thou visitest him?
For Thou hast made him a little lower than the angels.
And hast crowned him with glory and honor.

Thou madest him to have dominion over the works of thy hands;
Thou hast put all things under his feet:

PSALM 8:3-6

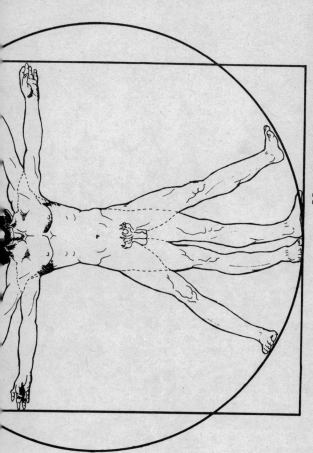

Man is Nature's sole mistake.

W. S. GILBERT

27

what the coyote made

MIWOK

The coyote called a council of animals to decide how man should be made. The mountain lion spoke first. He said, "I think that it is very important for man to have a loud voice like I do. And he might as well also have sharp claws, long fangs, and beautiful hair like I do."

The grizzly bear answered, "One loud voice like yours is all we need in this world. How will we ever have peace if we create another animal as noisy as you! I think men should be nice and quiet like me."

The buck replied, "I agree. He does not need to be able to roar. What he does need is a magnificent head of antlers. He also needs keen eyes and ears."

The coyote then got up and said that they were all stupid. "There is no sense at all," he complained, "in making man if he is going to be just like someone else. We should take the best points from every animal and put them all together. Man could have a loud voice, but should not use it all the time. He should be able to stand upright like the grizzly. He should have eyes and ears like the buck. But most important of all, he should be clever like me!"

But after the coyote spoke, the other animals all started shouting their disagreements and soon were in a fight. Finally everyone sat down by himself and started molding man out of clay. But night came and everyone except the coyote fell asleep. He stayed awake until he was finished and that is why man turned out the way the coyote wanted him to.

29

Our ancestry is firmly rooted in the animal world, and to its subtle, antique ways our hearts are yet pledged. Children of all animal kind, we inherited many a social nicety as well as the predator's way. But most significant of all our gifts, as things turned out, was the legacy bequeathed us by those killer apes, our immediate forebears. Even in the long days of our beginnings we held in our hand the weapon, an instrument somewhat older than ourselves.

ROBERT ARDREY

The question is this: is man an ape or an angel? I am on the side of the angels. I repudiate with indignation and abhorrence these newfangled theories.

BENJAMIN DISRAELI

Man is at bottom a wild, terrific animal. We know him only in connection with the taming and training, which is called civilization.

ARTHUR SCHOPENHAUER

Mother Earth and Father Sky lay together and conceived all beings, but they were not ready for creation yet. So they assumed human forms and talked together. They prepared the land for the coming of the creatures by bringing rain and corn to earth and planting corn in the sky to serve as guiding stars.

At last, in the innermost womb of Mother Earth, life began to appear. The first forms of life were wormlike crawling creatures. Only one of these creatures was able to find his way out of the deep darkness of the fourth womb. He went through the inner paths and finally came to the light of the sun. There he prayed to the Sun Father for all of the other things that were still inside the inner womb.

The Sun Father created two twins who were to finish his work of creation. The twins crawled back into the womb on spiderweb threads and began to teach the newly created beings so they would be prepared for a world of light. When they were ready, the twins made a ladder of vines and trees and made the creatures climb it. The second womb in which they arrived was much larger, but still dark. Here the people increased rapidly and soon were ready to climb the ladder to the third world. As they climbed this time, the twins separated them into different groups: yellow, brown-gray, red, white, black, and all colors mixed.

Finally they arrived in the birth channel of the earth. Here they were warned about the coming light of the sun, but were still not prepared for its brilliance. They came up at night and were certain that the Star Sirius was the sun. When morning came they were terrified at the great light. But gradually they learned to love the light and to grow into wise and thankful people under the warm rays of the sun.

ZUNI

31

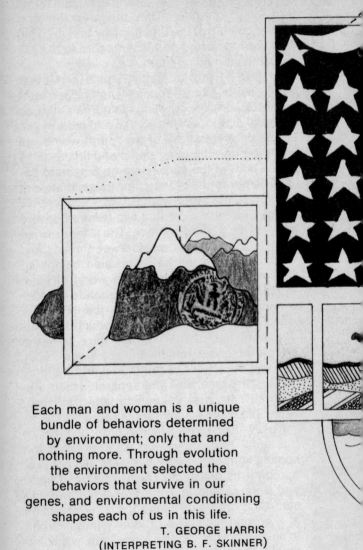

Each man and woman is a unique
bundle of behaviors determined
by environment; only that and
nothing more. Through evolution
the environment selected the
behaviors that survive in our
genes, and environmental conditioning
shapes each of us in this life.
                    T. GEORGE HARRIS
        (INTERPRETING B. F. SKINNER)

A small part of the universe is enclosed within a human skin.

B. F. SKINNER

MAN AND BEAST

It would probably be presumptuous to see Indian stories of man's developing from animals as being a scientific account of evolution. However, most American Indian mythologies did show man as being so closely related to animals that it is frequently difficult to distinguish animal characters from humans.

Western Europeans were, and to a certain extent still are, horrified by the suggestion that man is a descendant of apelike creatures and still retains many animal-like qualities. But the American Indians found many admirable qualities in their little brothers. They admired the cleverness of the coyote, the swiftness of the deer, the strength of the bear, and the pride of the eagle. Their mythology provided a basis for a friendly, ecological relationship with the animals which they were forced to kill for food and clothing but still respected, while the white men who tried to deny their animal ancestry ruthlessly and savagely destroyed buffalo and deer, exhibiting the very qualities that they so abhorred in the animal kingdom.

gold, silver, iron, and clay

Saturn (Cronus) created the first man. Man was made of gold and he was perfect and happy. There was no warfare and all was peace and joy on earth.

But in heaven, Jupiter (Zeus) took over control from his father Saturn and banished him to Tartarus. Jupiter created men of silver, and made their lives harder. They were forced to bear the cold of winter and work for their food, for Jupiter had created the four seasons. These men were not religious and Jupiter did not give them eternal life.

The race of silver did not last and they were followed by men made of brass. These men were warriors who battled against each other continually.

The final age was an age of iron. These were the worst of all men, for they were greedy and dug up from the earth all the treasures that had been hidden there and used them to make weapons of war.

Jupiter became angry with this degenerate race and decided to send a flood to destroy mankind. Rains poured down from heaven, and Neptune sent the waters of the ocean raging over the earth and all were destroyed, except for one man and one woman. Deucalion, son of Prometheus, and his wife Pyrrha, daughter of Epimetheus, were both very good, virtuous, and pious people. They had floated to the top of Mount Parnassus in a box, and when Jupiter saw that they were the only two people who were still alive, he decided to stop the flood and let them live.

35

Gradually they climbed to a temple and gave thanks to the gods and prayed for guidance. They received a strange message from the oracle. "Leave the temple with your head veiled and your clothes unbound and throw behind you the bones of your mother."

Pyrrha was horrified by this advice which sounded so disrespectful. But Deucalion finally said, "I think I understand it. Our mother is the earth and her bones are stones."

So the pair obeyed the oracle and cast the stones behind them. The stones that were thrown slowly began to take on human forms, and a final race of man was created from stone.

prometheus the fire bringer

Prometheus, a Titan who had helped Zeus against Cronus, was given the job of creating man and the animals for earth. Epimetheus, his brother, was to help.

Epimetheus began on the lower animals and became so excited with them that he gave away all of the good gifts of courage, wisdom, swiftness, warm coats, powerful claws, and wings.

Prometheus came to find what Epimetheus was doing and was very disturbed that there was nothing left for man. Since man must be better than the animals, there was nothing to do but make him like the gods.

So Prometheus took some earth and water and shaped man to look like the gods. He made him to stand upright so that he could look up at the stars instead of the earth. But he could not give man the powers of the gods, and the new creature was still too weak to rule over the world as he was supposed to.

At last, in desperation, Prometheus went to heaven and lit a torch at the chariot of the sun and brought to man the gift of fire. With the fire he brought men civilization and the ability to warm their homes and make weapons.

Zeus was furious at Prometheus, for he felt that man was now too powerful and might threaten the gods. So he created woman, Pandora, to weaken man and cause him trouble.

As for Prometheus, Zeus bound him to a rock on Mount Caucasus. There he was tormented for ages by a vulture who preyed on his liver, which was continually replenished, so that the torture would continue forever.

37

At last, however, Prometheus was freed. Some stories say that Hercules decided that freeing Prometheus would be the greatest deed man could do and with his mighty strength killed the vulture and broke the chains. Another myth says that the centaur Chron, after being wounded and in great pain, offered to die in Prometheus' place and so free the hero.

coyote the fire bringer

At the beginning of time, people had no fire. They were cold and had to eat their salmon raw. The only fire was on top of a high mountain guarded by evil spirits or "skookums." One day the coyote came to visit the people.

"Coyote," the people said, "we are miserable. Could you please get us fire from the mountains?"

"I will see what I can do," said the coyote.

He went up to the mountains to watch the skookums. He saw that one always guarded the fire while the others slept. When her turn was up, the skookum guarding the fire would say, "Sister, come and guard the fire." It usually took a little while for the new guard to come. The coyote thought that he could steal the fire, but he was afraid that the skookums would catch him before he could get to the bottom of the mountain, because the skookums could run very fast. At last he thought of a plan.

The next day, the coyote called all of the animals together and stationed them in a relay up the mountain. Then he went to the top and waited for the guards to change. At last he heard the skookum guarding the fire say, "Sister, come and guard the fire." Without waiting at all, the coyote jumped up and grabbed a piece of wood carrying the fire.

Down the mountain he ran, but the skookums were right behind him. They caught up with him just as he reached the treeline. One of the skookums grabbed his tail and it turned

39

black. But he had reached the cougar, and passed the flaming torch on to him.

The cougar passed the brand on to the fox, who passed it on to the squirrel. The fire burned a black spot on the squirrel's back and made his tail curl. But he reached the edge of the forest in time to give the fire to the antelope.

The antelope was such a swift runner that all the animals were sure the skookums would tire out. But they didn't. At last the antelope collapsed from exhaustion. There was only a coal left, and a small frog grabbed the coal and swallowed it.

The skookums were right behind. One of them caught the frog by the tail. The frog gave a mighty leap and his tail pulled right off, and since that time frogs have had no tails.

But finally, the frog was exhausted, too. Not knowing what to do, he spat out the coal onto some wood. The wood swallowed it. The skookums came up just as the coal disappeared into the wood. They stood a long time staring. But they did not know how to get the fire back out of the wood. At last they left and went back up the mountain.

Then the coyote ran up joyfully. He knew how to get the fire out of the wood. He took two pieces of wood and rubbed them together.

From that day on, people have had fire to heat their homes and to cook their salmon.

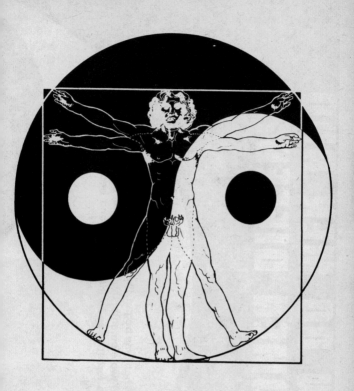

IN THE BEGINNING, from nothing or stone or clay or
the body of god, through pain and sacrifice, were
created the universe and man—its crowning achievement
or its greatest mistake.

And with this creation came the eternally conflicting,
intermeshing, and cooperating pairs of opposites which
keep the universe in motion and which man must
understand and assimilate to be at peace with himself.
Male and female. Good and evil. War and peace. Life
and death.

41

HOW DO MEN AND WOMEN DIFFER?

When time began, the eternal Tao separated into two elements; the light, spiritual, masculine forces rose to the heavens and became yang.

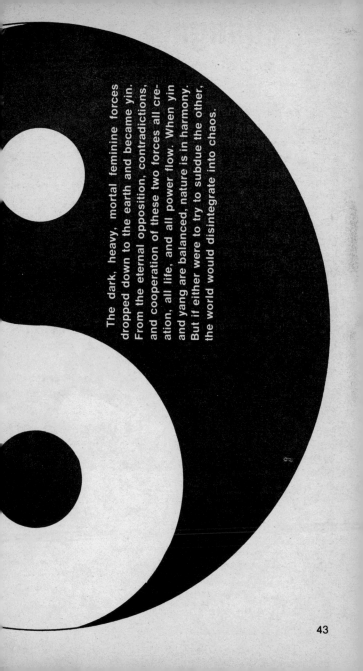

The dark, heavy, mortal feminine forces dropped down to the earth and became yin. From the eternal opposition, contradictions, and cooperation of these two forces all creation, all life, and all power flow. When yin and yang are balanced, nature is in harmony. But if either were to try to subdue the other, the world would disintegrate into chaos.

changing woman

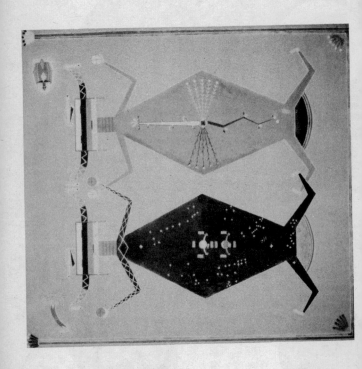

In the great desert of multicolored sand stood the Mountain-Around-Which-Moving-Was-Done, and at the foot of this great mountain was found a baby girl.

First Man and First Woman found the child when the earth was still unformed and incomplete. They took her home with them and raised her carefully, and the gods smiled on her and loved her. As she grew into womanhood, the world itself reached maturity as the mountains and valleys were all put into the proper places.

At last she was grown and the world was complete, and to celebrate her becoming a woman, the gods gave her a Blessing Way, Walking-into-Beauty. Songs and chants were sung to her, and her body was shaped with a sacred stick so that it would grow strong and beautiful. Each morning of the ceremony, she ran to greet the sun as it arose. The sacred ceremony was preserved and it is now given to all Navajo girls when they reach adulthood.

But the young girl did not stay the same. Each winter she became withered and white-haired, just as the earth became bare and snow-covered. But each spring as the colors of life grew back on the land, the colors of youth and beauty appeared in her cheeks and in her hair. So she is called Changing Woman, or "A Woman She Becomes Time and Again."

The sun fell in love with Changing Woman, but she did not know what to do with him. So she went to First Woman for advice. On the advice of First Woman, she met the sun and he made love to her. Nine months later, twin sons were born to her and she raised them with love and care. For monsters had now ap-

45

peared in the world, and the people were being destroyed. Changing Woman hoped her sons could save the world from the monsters.

When the twin boys were grown, Changing Woman sent them to the sun, their father, to get power from him so that they could fight the monsters. After undergoing severe tests by their father, the boys returned and destroyed all of the monsters.

Now the world was complete and the monsters were dead. It was a perfect place for people, but there were very few left. Changing Woman pondered over this problem, and at last she took two baskets of corn. One was of white corn and one was of yellow corn. From the white cornmeal she shaped a man and from the yellow cornmeal she shaped a woman.

And so the earth was populated again, a changing world and a beautiful world—the world of Changing Woman.

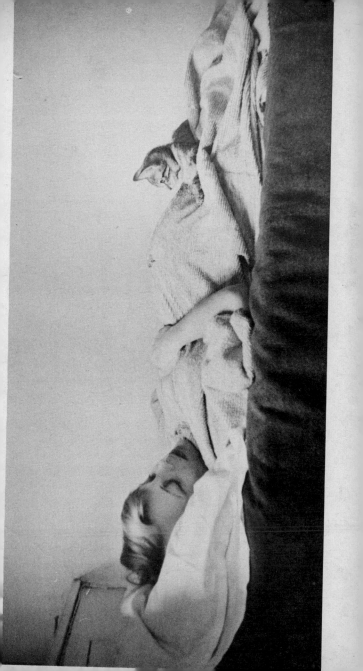

In almost all cultures, the male is associated with the sky or sun and represents light and spirit. The female is associated with the earth and the dark and mysterious depths that bring forth

The spirit of the Fountain dies
not.
It is called the Mysterious
Feminine.
The Doorway of the Mysterious
Feminine
Is called the Root of
Heaven-and-Earth

THE TAO TE CHING

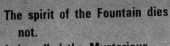

In the Zuñi creation myth, the
earth is pictured as a huge womb
where all of life is created and
follows the birth channel to be
eventually born.

The Ephesians pictured their great woman goddess—variously known as Cybele, Artemis, or Diana—as a warm mother with enough breasts to suckle all of her young.

But Mother Earth who gives life is also the final resting place of the dead, and the Polynesians show this beautifully in their myth of Hine Titama, who was the mother of all mankind, but also the bringer of death to man.

sati and siva

When creation was completed, two pairs of the divine trinity, Brahma and his wife, Sarasvati, and Vishnu and his wife, Lakshmi, were working hard in their roles as creators and preservers of the world. But high on a lofty mountain in the Himalayas, Siva sat alone meditating, refusing to become involved in the affairs of the world. Brahma and Vishnu became worried. Siva's role as destroyer of the old and worn-out was essential to the functioning of the world. If he could not be induced to take a wife and assume his job as destroyer, the world would stagnate and turn into a huge trash pile.

Sarasvati and Lakshmi looked eagerly for a woman who would be worthy of being Siva's partner. Only Makashakti, the Great Mother herself, could fulfill the role. So at the urging of the four great gods, the Great Mother incarnated herself as Sati, the daughter of the sage Dakshi. Knowing from the time of her birth that she was destined to be the wife of Siva, she devoted herself to the practice of yoga and to agonizing austerities so that she might be worthy of him.

But Sati's father disliked Siva, for he was thin and pale from his life of yoga and wore beggar's rags and dead men's bones. Dakshi was angry that his daughter was imitating Siva in meditation and austerities. Perhaps, he thought, if she were married and had a family she would act more normal. So all of the handsome and wealthy men in the country were invited to Dakshi's home so Sati could choose a husband. Sati walked unhappily through the ranks of brave princes decked in gold and jewels and found none that appealed to her.

For hours she walked among the men, carrying the wreath she was to give to the man she chose, and at last her father and all of the suitors became tired of her procrastination.

"There is no one else coming," her father said angrily. "So hurry up and make your choice. You are embarrassing me before the most powerful men in the country!"

In desperation Sati threw the wreath into the air and cried, "Siva, take me, for I will have no other!"

And the great miracle occurred. The powerful yogi left his spot on the mountain and took the wreath and his bride.

It is woman who seduced man from his spiritual quest to enjoy the pleasures of the world. But it is woman, herself, who is the goal of man's quest.

Now that Siva had found a woman he could love, he became the most devoted of husbands, and the couple spent the years in lovemaking and sharing together in meditation.

But Sati was not quite Siva's equal in meditation, and occasionally she became tired and would slip off to rest. One day she was feeling very playful so she skipped up behind Siva and put her hands over his eyes. Immediately the world plunged into darkness. Horrified, Sati started to take her hands off, but before she could, a third eye suddenly appeared in Siva's forehead. It gave off such tremendous power that all of the forests were burned black.

Sati fell down weeping over the horrible ruin that her joke had caused, and Siva, who could not bear her tears, gave the trees back their life and caused new leaves to spring on their branches. But the third eye which appeared in his forehead remained to give him power.

After several years, Sati's father planned a great festival and invited all of the gods except Siva and Sati. Sati and Siva were both furious at this insult, and they decided to go anyway. When they arrived at the festival, they found a great fire burning which Dakshi had built for the renewing of the universe. Without warning, Sati rushed into the middle of the gathering and, before the eyes of all the horrified spectators, cast herself into the fire!

Siva ran after her, but he was too late. All he took out of the fire was a blackened body. Crazed with grief, he began dancing a dance of grief. Over the heavens and through the mountains he danced with the charred body of his beloved, and as he danced, the tides and the winds began to beat in time to the rhythm of Siva's feet. Brahma watched aghast as Siva's dance of mourning began to slowly evolve into the dance of destruction which would end the created world and cause all to be absorbed into the World Spirit.

But it was not time for the world to end. Vishnu, the preserver, had to stop the crazed Siva. Vishnu rushed after Siva and began to cut the charred body of Sati into thousands of pieces, dropping them in the various parts of India. By now Siva was so involved in his dance that he did not even notice, until at last Sati was gone. Siva suddenly realized that his beloved had disappeared, and turned around to face the sorrowful Vishnu.

"You cannot stop the world because you have lost your wife," Vishnu said. "You know that she is immortal and will reappear in another form."

Siva did not reply, but stopped his dance and returned to his long-interrupted meditations on the mountains.

Sati, Parvati, and Kali. Siva can appear in only one form, but woman is so many-faceted and confusing that it seems impossible to express all of her confusing and conflicting attributes in one person.

After many years, Siva was again needed in the world and so Sati was reborn as Parvati. Again she grew to womanhood knowing that she was Siva's intended, but having already known his love, she did not think that she would need to meditate to gain power over him. So she grew up a beautiful and talented girl, but Siva showed no interest in her. Parvati and the gods used every trick they could think of to attract Siva's attention, but he might as well have been blind. He apparently did not even know that she existed.

Finally, in despair, the gods called Kama, the god of love. Kama shot an arrow at Siva, but Siva was so angry at being disturbed that he turned the full force of his third eye on Kama and burned him to a crisp.

Now the gods were really upset, and Parvati was so worried that she began to undergo the most extreme penances possible. She vowed not to eat and to lie in ice water and torture herself until Siva would marry her.

Siva finally awakened from his meditation and finally noticed the beautiful girl who was rapidly becoming emaciated from her self-tortures. So he took the form of Brahma and went down to talk to her.

"Why are you destroying your beautiful body?" he asked.

"So that I will be worthy of my Lord Siva," was her reply.

"Worthy of him?" laughed Siva in Brahma's form. "He is old, ugly, and bad-tempered, and he spends all of his time in cemeteries. What do you want with him?"

But Parvati put her hands over her ears and refused to listen to anything against Siva. Then Siva appeared to her in his own form and married her.

Parvati and Siva again spent many years in conjugal bliss, but Siva's spouse had to assume still other forms in order to assist him in all his jobs. Siva's primary role is the destruction of the old universe, and when she helps him with this task, Sati/Parvati appears as Kali, a terrible form wearing a necklace of skulls and drinking blood.

Kali first appeared to kill the demon Raktavira, who was so powerful that every drop of his blood that was shed would produce thousands of new demons. To save the world from his cruelty, Kali killed him and drank his blood as it fell. But from this combat she gained a love of blood and destruction.

As Kali, she dances with Siva to bring in the end of the age. But so excited she is by blood and destruction that she sometimes tries to start the dance too early. One time she began the great dance of destruction long before its time. Already she had slaughtered all of the evil demons and was ready to start on the gods. Siva rushed to her in desperation to stop her, but she was so crazed that she didn't even see him. Soon she was dancing on top of Siva himself, and only then did she come to her senses. Contrite after this treatment of her lover, she now waits patiently with Siva for the day of destruction to come at the proper time.

One quiet afternoon Ramakrishna beheld a
beautiful woman ascend from the Ganges
and approach the grove in which he was
meditating. He perceived that she was
about to give birth to a child. In a moment,
the babe was born, and she gently nursed
it. Presently, however, she assumed a
horrible aspect, took the infant in her now
ugly jaws and crushed and chewed it.
Swallowing it, she returned again to the
Ganges, where she disappeared.

THE GOSPEL OF SRI RAMAKRISHNA

In 1861 J. J. Bachofen wrote a book called *Mutterrecht* (Mother Right) in which he suggested that early human societies were ruled by women and generally worshipped female deities. These mother goddesses represented Mother Earth and were worshipped primarily in connection with planting and harvest. Matriarchal cultures and religions had reverence for the earth and the animals which were also children of the earth.

Bachofen believed that these societies were eventually overthrown by men who set up a patriarchal government and religion, ruled by men and having male gods. The patriarchal culture introduced law by force, technology, a desire for achievement, and an attempt to improve upon the world. In order to secure their control, patriarchal societies subjugated women and held them as inferiors in fear that they would again become powerful.

Bachofen showed that the difference between the patriarchal and the matriarchal order went far beyond the social supremacy of men and women, respectively, but was one of social and moral principles. Matriarchal culture is characterized by an emphasis on ties of blood, ties to the soil, and a passive acceptance of all natural phenomena. Patriarchal society, in contrast, is characterized by respect for man-made law, by a predominance of rational thought, and by man's effort to change natural phenomena. Insofar as these principles are concerned, the patriarchal culture constitutes a definite progress over the matriarchal world. In other respects, however, the matriarchal principles were superior to the victorious patriarchal ones. In the matriarchal concept all men are equal, since they are all the children of mothers and each one a child of Mother Earth. A mother loves all her children alike and without conditions, since her

59

love is based on the fact that they are her children and not on any particular merit or achievement; the aim of life is the happiness of men, and there is nothing more important or dignified than human existence and life. The patriarchal system, on the other hand, considers obedience to authority to be the main virtue. Instead of the principle of equality, we find the concept of the favorite son and a hierarchical order in society. from Erich Fromm *The Forgotten Language*

marduk and tiamat

In the beginning were the sweet male waters, Apsu, and the female salt waters, Tiamat. They contained within themselves the seeds of life and they brought into being the gods.

The new gods were noisy and Apsu could not rest, so he decided to destroy them. But one of the new gods, Ea, heard of the plot and bound Apsu and killed him.

Tiamat, in fury, created eleven more gods to help her against the murderers of Apsu. But Marduk, the male child of the sun, prepared to lead the gods against their mother. The other gods promised to give Marduk supreme power if he could kill Tiamat.

Marduk, armed with the wind and a thunderbolt, attacked the monster Tiamat and, after a tremendous fight, killed her.

He cut her body in two and from the two halves he made the heavens and the earth. As for the gods that had aided Tiamat, Marduk put them in the sky as the signs of the zodiac.

Technology represents the male attitude in most mythologies, and cultures with a strong patriarchal religion seem to be intent on enslaving and controlling the female powers of Mother Earth. Man mines the minerals from the earth, constructs cities and roads, develops machines to do his work, and even attempts to control the weather.

Ecology seems to be the female attitude toward the earth. Cultures that worship Mother Earth see themselves as her children and have a profound respect for her. Their homes fit into the landscape, and both planting and harvesting are done with prayer and reverence, according to the rhythms of nature.

In time grasses will poke through the asphalt and trees will split the concrete;
and we who think we have overpowered and gutted and raped the land and polluted the skies and the water
will find that nature allowed us this moment of play as part of her experiment.

RAY ALSBURY

adam and eve

HEBREW

The Lord God took the man and put him in the Garden of Eden to till it and keep it. And the Lord God commanded the man saying, "You may freely eat of every tree of the garden; but of the tree of knowledge of good and evil you shall not eat, for in the day that you eat of it you shall die."

Then the Lord God said, "It is not good that the man should be alone; I will make him a helper fit for him." So out of the ground the Lord God formed every beast of the field and every bird of the air, and brought them to the man to see what he would call them; and whatever the man called every living creature, that was its name. The man gives names to all cattle, and to the birds of the air, and to every beast of the field; but for the man there was not found a helper fit for him. So the Lord God caused a deep sleep to fall upon the man, and while he slept he took one of his ribs and closed up its place with flesh; and the rib which the Lord God had taken from the man he made into a woman and brought her to the man. Then the man said, "This at last is bone of my bones and flesh of my flesh; she shall be called Woman, because she was taken out of Man."

Therefore a man leaves his father and his mother and cleaves to his wife, and they become one flesh. And the man and his wife were both naked, and were not ashamed.

Now the serpent was more subtle than any other wild creature that the Lord God had made. He said to the woman, "Did God say, 'You shall not eat of any tree of the garden'?" And the woman said to the serpent, "We may eat of the fruit of the trees of the garden; but God said, *'You shall not eat of the fruit of the tree which is in the midst of the garden, neither shall you touch it, lest you die.'* " But the serpent said to the woman, "You will not die. For God knows that when you eat of it your eyes will be opened, and you will be like God, knowing good and evil." So when the woman saw that the tree was good for food, and that it was a delight to the eyes, and that the tree was to be desired to make one wise, she took of its fruit and ate; and she also gave some to her husband, and he ate. Then the eyes of both were opened, and they knew that they were naked; and they sewed fig leaves together and made themselves aprons.

And they heard the sound of the Lord God walking in the garden in the cool of the day, and the man and his wife hid themselves from the presence of the Lord God among the trees of the garden. But the Lord God called to the man, and said to him, *"Where are you?"* And he said, "I heard the sound of thee in the garden, and I was afraid, because I was naked, and I hid myself." He said, *"Who told you that you were naked?* Have you eaten of the tree of which I commanded you not to eat?" The man said, "The woman whom thou gavest to be with me, she gave me fruit of the tree, and I ate." Then the Lord God said to the woman, *"What is this that you have done?"* The woman said, "The serpent beguiled me, and I ate." The Lord God said to the serpent,

"Because you have done this,
      cursed are you above all cattle;
      and above all wild animals,
upon your belly you shall go,
      and dust you shall eat
      all the days of your life.
I will put enmity between you and the
      woman,
      and between your seed and her seed;
he shall bruise your head,
      and you shall bruise his heel."
To the woman he said,
      "I will greatly multiply your pain in child-
            bearing;
      yet your desire shall be for your hus-
            band,
      and he shall rule over you."
And to Adam he said,
      "Because you have listened to the voice
            of your wife,
      and have eaten of the tree of which
            I commanded you,
      'You shall not eat of it,'
cursed is the ground because of you;
      in toil you shall eat of it all the days
            of your life;
      thorns and thistles it shall bring forth to
            you;
      and you shall eat the plants of the field.
In the sweat of your face you shall eat
            bread
      till you return to the ground, for out
            of it you were taken;
      you are dust,
      and to dust you shall return."
The man called his wife's name Eve, because
she was the mother of all living. And the Lord
God made for Adam and for his wife garments
of skins, and clothed them.

Then the Lord God said, *"Behold, the man has become like one of us, knowing good and evil; and now, lest he put forth his hand and take also of the tree of life, and eat, and live forever"*—therefore the Lord God sent him forth from the Garden of Eden, to till the ground from which he was taken. He drove out the man; and at the east of the Garden of Eden he placed the cherubim, and a flaming sword which turned every way, to guard the way to the tree of life.

GENESIS 2:15-25;3:1-24

Do you know that each of you women is an Eve? The sentence of God on this sex of yours lives in this age; the guilt must necessarily live too. You are the gate of hell, you are the temptress of the forbidden tree; you are the first deserter of the divine law.

TERTULLIAN

from the woman's bible

Note the significant fact that we always hear of the "fall of man," not the fall of woman, showing that the consensus of human thought has been more unerring than masculine interpretation. Reading this narrative carefully, it is amazing that any set of men ever claimed that the dogma of the inferiority of woman is here set forth. The conduct of Eve from the beginning to the end is so superior to that of Adam. The command not to eat of the fruit of the tree of Knowledge was given to the man alone before woman was formed. Genesis ii, 17. Therefore the injunction was not brought to Eve with the impressive solemnity of a Divine Voice, but whispered to her by her husband and equal. It was a serpent supernaturally endowed, a seraphim as Scott and other commentators have claimed, who talked with Eve, and whose words might reasonably seem superior to the second-hand story of her companion—nor does the woman yield at once. She quotes the command not to eat of the fruit to which the serpent replies "Dying ye shall not die," v. 4, literal translation. In other words telling her that if the mortal body does perish, the immortal part shall live forever, and offering as the reward of her act the attainment of Knowledge.

Then the woman, fearless of death if she can gain wisdom, takes of the fruit; and all this time Adam standing beside her interposes no word of objection. "Her husband with her" are the words of v. 6. Had he been the representative of the divinely appointed head in married life, he assuredly would have taken upon himself the burden of the discussion with the serpent, but no, he is silent in this crisis of their fate. Having had the command from God himself he interposes no word of warning or remonstrance, but takes the fruit from the hand of his wife without a protest. It takes six verses to describe the "fall" of woman, the fall of man is contemptuously dismissed in a line and a half.

The subsequent conduct of Adam was to the last degree dastardly. When the awful time of reckoning comes, and the Jehovah God appears to demand why his command has been disobeyed, Adam endeavors to shield himself behind the gentle being he has declared to be so dear. "The woman thou gavest to be with me, she gave me and I did eat," he whines—trying to shield himself at his wife's expense! Again we are amazed that upon such a story men have built up a theory of their superiority!

LILLIE DEVEREUX BLAKE

WAS NIETZSCHE His FIRST?
—FELICiA

Woman is God's second mistake.
—Nietzsche

"Prometheus has destroyed us," Zeus confided morosely to Hephaestus. "He has made man too powerful by giving him the gift of fire and the skill to use it to make weapons. Our little creature is likely to destroy us someday."

"There must be some way we could make him weaker," Hephaestus replied. And for a long time the two gods pondered the problem. Then Hera, Zeus' quarrelsome wife, walked by the door and Zeus snapped his fingers with glee.

"I know," he said, "let's make a woman for man!"

Hephaestus, the master craftsman, immediately set to work and soon fashioned a beautiful woman out of clay. The gods, who were delighted with Zeus' scheme, gave her all of their gifts of beauty, charm, and grace, but also filled her with lies, treachery, and deceit. They also gave her an urn filled with all the diseases, natural calamities, and evils that could plague mankind and warned her never to look inside it. Then they dressed her in beautiful clothes and sent her to Epimetheus, his brother, because Prometheus had already been bound on Mount Caucasus in punishment for giving man fire.

Epimetheus was true to his name "After-Thought" and did not even think once before accepting this beautiful woman from his enemy.

Pandora had scarcely entered her new home before she was overcome with curiosity about the mysterious urn which she had been warned not to open. She tried hard to busy herself entertaining her new husband and decorating the house, but the strange urn was never out of her thoughts for more than a few minutes.

At last, one day when Epimetheus was gone, Pandora could not restrain herself any longer.

She went into the room with the urn and picked it up, thinking she would only take a little peek.

But as soon as the lid was off, a horrible cloud of noisy, evil beings flew up into the air and scattered over the whole earth. Pandora clapped the lid back on immediately, but it was too late. All of man's miseries had been let loose on the world.

But there was something else in the urn. Pandora could hear a fluttering against the walls. Again her curiosity overcame her and she decided that surely nothing worse could happen, so she opened the lid again.

A small, butterfly-like being that fluttered out and rested on her shoulder emerged. It was hope, one final gift of the gods. But whether it was good or evil, man has not yet decided.

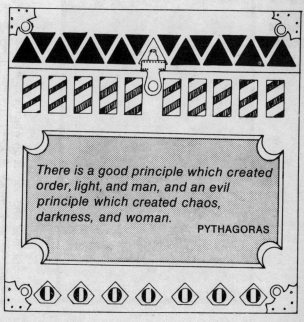

There is a good principle which created order, light, and man, and an evil principle which created chaos, darkness, and woman.

PYTHAGORAS

izanagi and izanami

JAPANESE

Out of chaos and confusion which existed before the worlds began, pairs of gods and goddesses began to appear. The eighth pair were a brother and sister named Izanagi and Izanami. To them was given the task of creating the world. The other gods and goddesses gave Izanagi a miraculous lance which he was to use in creation. So the brother and sister walked out on the Floating Bridge of Heaven and Izanagi plunged his lance into the chaos below. Gradually the matter began to come together at the tip of the lance. When Izanagi was satisfied that he had given enough order to the world below, he lifted the lance and drops of water fell from it. These became the island of Onokoro.

Excited by the new land which they had created, the pair descended to the island and began to explore it. Izanagi went to the left and Izanami went to the right. Both were filled with awe and joy at the beauty they saw around them.

Suddenly they met face to face on the other island, and Izanami exclaimed, "Oh, what a handsome man!" ignoring the convention that men should speak first. Izanagi also cried out, "Oh, what a beautiful woman!"

So there on the shore of the island they had created, the god and goddess fell in love. Soon Izanami had a child. But something was wrong. The child was hideously deformed.

Discouraged by their monster-child, the couple returned over the Floating Bridge of Heaven to ask the older gods what had gone wrong. The reply was quick and sober.

"Things are out of order in your world. You have a woman who thinks she is a man and speaks first."

Izanami immediately remembered the trip around the island when she had exclaimed in admiration of her husband. She was contrite and embarrassed about the incident and begged to know how she could right things.

The gods suggested that the two go back to the time when they had first descended to the island and repeat the whole ritual, but with Izanagi speaking first.

The two did as they were told, and this time they had beautiful children. This time their children included the other islands, the wind, the trees, and the mountains. And from this time on, woman has not tried to upset the order of the world by thinking that she can be a man.

75

woman must be obedient

There was once a man who had a very beautiful daughter named Nkoyo. But she was also very spoiled and disobedient and refused to marry any of the fine young men her father found for her.

One day a skull from the Bush of Ghosts heard of Nkoyo's beauty and decided he wanted to marry her. However, he knew that she would not marry a skull, so he went to all of his friends and borrowed various parts of the body. He chose only those parts of the body that were most perfect and handsome, borrowing a face from one friend and arms from another. By the time he was ready to visit Nkoyo, he had the most handsome body in the country.

As soon as he got to town, Nkoyo heard about the handsome stranger, and the moment she caught sight of him she fell in love with him. Her parents did not want her to marry a stranger, but she was so insistent that they finally gave in. As soon as they were married, the skull said, "I must be returning to my home in a far country and Nkoyo must come with me."

Nkoyo's father took her aside and said, "I still do not like the looks of this man, but you must go with your husband. Let me give you one piece of advice, though. Do not be as disobedient and stubborn in your new home as you have been here."

At first Nkoyo enjoyed the journey, but as they approached the Bush of Ghosts, she became rather apprehensive. At last they came

76

to the home of one of the skull's friends from whom he had borrowed his arms. The skull said, "We must stop here to return something I have borrowed."

Nkoyo was very frightened when her husband returned without arms. But she was more frightened when they stopped at the next house and returned his feet, then his legs, then his torso, and finally his face, and she discovered that her handsome husband was only a skull.

There was no way of escape. The unhappy girl had to go with the husband she had chosen. At last they arrived at his home, and Nkoyo found that she had to take care of the skull's invalid mother.

By now Nkoyo was sorry that she had been so willful and remembered her father's advice. So she was a very obedient wife and took very good care of her mother-in-law.

One day the grateful mother-in-law came to Nkoyo quietly. "I have heard a rumor," she said, "that the people of the Bush of Ghosts have heard that a living person is here. They are planning to come tonight to kill you and

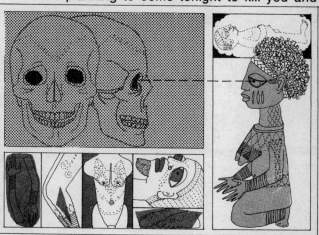

eat you. But since you have been so good to me, I will help you escape to your parents' home. However, I will only let you go if you will promise never to be disobedient again. I hope you have learned by now that good looks and love are very fleeting."

Nkoyo eagerly promised that she would never again disobey her parents, and her mother-in-law called up a wind which blew her back to her home.

The whole town rejoiced at Nkoyo's return, for they had learned that her husband was a skull. As for Nkoyo, she married the man her parents had chosen for her and became known throughout the village as the model of an obedient wife.

what does woman want?

Despite my 30 years of research into the feminine soul, I have not yet been able to answer ... the great question that has never been answered:

What does a woman want?

—Freud

King Arthur one day was hunting in the woods when suddenly he met a well-armed knight who stopped him and challenged him to fight.

"But I am not armed," protested Arthur.

"All right, then," replied the knight, "I will give you a chance to escape according to your rules of chivalry. I will give you a riddle to solve and a year in which to solve it. Next year at this time you must return to this same spot, again unarmed, and give me the answer to my riddle. If you fail, then I can kill you without violating your code. The riddle is, 'What is the thing that women desire most?' "

Arthur pledged to return and went back to his castle quite disturbed. Sir Gawaine noticed how upset he was and asked what the problem was. Arthur explained what had happened.

"That is no problem at all," said Sir Gawaine. "All we have to do is ask some women. Surely we will get the answer very quickly."

"That is a very good idea," said King Arthur. "Let's both travel throughout the country and ask for answers. We can write down all of the answers in a book so that we will not forget any."

So both traveled through the country for several months. But the quest turned out to be more difficult than it had appeared at first. All of the women said something different. The young women wanted husbands, married women wanted to be rich, sick women wanted to be well, and old women wanted to be young again. There did not seem to be anything that all women wanted.

So when only one month remained in the year, King Arthur set off again. This time he came to a forest and found within it the ugliest hag that had ever been seen on the earth. King Arthur was so repelled by her appearance that he was going to ride right past her instead of asking for her answer, but she stood in the road and stopped him.

"Why are you riding so fast through the woods that you do not have time to greet a lonely woman?" she demanded.

"I am on an important quest," replied Arthur curtly, trying to get around her.

"And I know the only answer to the question you have been asked that can save your life," replied the hag slyly.

"Then tell me quickly," said Arthur.

"On one condition only. I would like to have a husband. And I think one of your knights would do fine. So I will tell you the answer to your question when you obtain the promise of one of your knights to marry me." With that she laughed and went into her cabin.

Arthur returned to the castle more dejected than ever. And again Gawaine asked him what the trouble was. As soon as Arthur told him, he immediately agreed to marry the hag.

"But you would not believe how ugly she is!" protested Arthur.

"It would be but a small price to pay for the life of my king," replied Gawaine. At last Arthur accepted his offer and returned to the hag.

"The answer is very simple," she replied. "What every woman wants is to have her way with men."

When the year was up, Arthur returned to the knight and first gave him all of the answers that he and Gawaine had collected.

"All of these answers are wrong," laughed the knight. "Are you ready to die?"

"Wait, I have one more answer," said Arthur. "What every woman wants is to have her way with men."

The knight walked away in fury. "It must have been my sister who told you," he muttered.

Arthur returned to Camelot rejoicing, but Sir Gawaine was forced to go to the forest to claim his bride.

As much of a gentleman as he was, Sir Gawaine had to use all of the self-control he had to keep from vomiting at the sight of his bride-to-be. But he greeted her courteously and returned with her to the court. There he submitted bravely to the mockery of the other knights and the townspeople, and took the hag to the chapel and married her.

Sir Gawaine maintained his knightly and courteous behavior until nighttime when he lay in bed with his bride. Then he could not bring himself to kiss her or even to look at her.

"What is the matter, my lord, that you do not do your duty as a husband?" asked the hag.

Sir Gawaine, who was truthful as well as courteous, replied, "I am very sorry, but I am upset by your age, your ugliness, and your low birth."

"You do wrong to be upset by these things," she replied. "For age brings discretion, and ugliness provides you security from all your rivals, and true quality does not depend upon birth but character."

Sir Gawaine was impressed by the wisdom of her reply and turned to face her again. But instead of the old hag who had been there before, he now saw a beautiful young lady.

"I see you are surprised," she laughed. "I have been enchanted by my evil stepmother. The enchantment could not be broken until a knight of the Round Table would wed me."

"But the charm is only half broken now," she went on. "I can only have my natural form for half of the day. I can either be a hag by night and beautiful during the day for the court to see, or I can be a hag by day and beautiful for you at night."

Sir Gawaine mused over this choice for a long time. Finally he said, "There are advantages to both and I cannot decide between them. I will let you make the choice. Let it be the way you desire, for my body and soul are yours."

Then the lady rejoiced. "Now I am free of the charm altogether. For the final test to break the spell was that the knight who married me must be willing to let me have my way with him."

The history of mankind is a history of repeated injuries and usurpations on the part of men toward women, having in direct object the establishment of an absolute tyranny over her. To prove this, let facts be submitted to a candid world.

He has never permitted her to exercise her inalienable right to the elective franchise.

He has compelled her to submit to laws, in the formation of which she has no voice . . .

Having deprived her of this first right of a citizen, the elective franchise, thereby leaving her without representation in the halls of legislation, he has oppressed her on all sides.

He has made her, if married, in the eye of the law, civilly dead. . . . In the covenant of marriage, she is compelled to promise obedience to her husband, he becoming, to all intents and purposes, her master—the law giving him power to deprive her of her liberty, and to administer chastisement.

. . . He has monopolized nearly all the profitable employments, and from those she is permitted to follow, she receives but a scanty remuneration. He closes against her all the avenues to wealth and distinction which he considers most honorable to himself. As a teacher of theology, medicine, or law, she is not known.

. . . He has created a false public sentiment by giving to the world a different code of morals for men and women, by which moral delinquencies which exclude women from society are not only tolerated but deemed of little account in men.

He has usurped the prerogative of Jehova himself, claiming it is his right to assign to her a sphere of action, when that belongs to her conscience and to her God . . .

He has endeavored, in every way he could, to destroy her confidence in her own powers, to lessen her self-respect, and to make her willing to lead an abject and dependent life.

THE SENECA FALLS DECLARATION OF RIGHTS AND SENTIMENTS, 1848

deirdre of the sorrows

IRISH

"Woe to this child," prophesied the soothsayer at Deirdre's birth, "for she shall be the ruin of all Ireland and the death of its three greatest heroes."

The tiny baby was so sweet and innocent that Felimid could almost laugh at these dire predictions. But his friends believed strongly in the soothsayer and at their urgings, Felimid sent his small daughter and a faithful nurse to live in a remote, isolated forest where she could never possibly have any effect on the fate of Ireland. So Deirdre grew up into the most beautiful woman of Ireland without ever seeing the face of a man. But word of her beauty leaked out of the forest and came to the castle of King Conchobar, who decided that if her beauty matched her reputation, he would marry her himself.

So the king sent for Deirdre and found that she was even more beautiful than he had imagined. But Deirdre was not at all impressed with Conchobar, for he was old and ugly, and although Deirdre had not seen many men in her secluded life, she was sure there had to be something better than this! That night Deirdre dreamed of a young and handsome man with hair like the raven, flesh like the snow, and cheeks as red as berries. "A man like that I could love," she thought.

The next day the king asked her to marry him. Deirdre replied that she was too young to be married, and begged the king to let her live in the forest for another year until she was old enough. The king was satisfied with her answer, and Deirdre and her nurse returned to the forest.

Deirdre thought little of the king she was betrothed to and instead spent all of her time dreaming of the man with the raven hair and cheeks like berries. The nurse listened to her musings in fear and worry. At last she said, "Deirdre, you must quit dreaming of a man like this, for I know one who fits the description. He is Naois, the son of Usnach, and I am sure that he is the man of the prophecy, for he and his two brothers are the greatest heroes of all Ireland. If you ever meet him, you will bring death to him and ruin to all of Ireland."

It was only a few days later that Deirdre heard a hunting horn. She ran to the window just in time to see three handsome men ride by, and one of them had hair like the raven, flesh like the snow, and cheeks as red as berries. "It is Naois," she cried.

"Don't be a fool," cried her nurse, struggling to hold Deirdre. "Let him go."

But Deirdre pulled free from the nurse and ran out into the forest after the three huntsmen. "Naois," she cried. "Don't leave me!"

"I heard something call," said Naois. "Let's go back."

"It was only the wind," said his two brothers, Ainle and Arden.

But again the call came. "Naois! Come back!"

"Don't go," said Arden. "I am afraid that this voice will bring evil."

But Naois could not resist the sweet voice he heard, and rode back toward the sound. As he came out of the forest onto a grassy

knoll beside a stream he saw the most beautiful woman in the world.

"Who are you?" he asked in awe. "Are you a woman or a fairy?"

"I am Deirdre," she replied.

Naois was struck with horror when he heard her name, for he, too, had heard the prophecy about Deirdre and he knew that she was betrothed to the king. But as he looked into her eyes, he knew that neither death, nor banishment, nor disloyalty could keep him from loving her.

When Ainle and Arden found their brother, he and Deirdre were already deep in a kiss of love. The two looked at each other in despair, for they knew that the prophecy meant their undoing as well as Naois's, but it took them only a minute to decide that they would never desert their brother.

Knowing that King Conchobar would never allow his beloved to marry another, the three brothers fled with Deirdre to another country. For several years they lived in peace, but they were all lonely for their homeland.

One day a messenger from King Conchobar arrived, bringing an invitation to the four of them to come to a feast. Hoping that this meant the end of their exile, the four young people eagerly accepted and returned to their beloved Ireland.

King Conchobar, too, hoped that they could return in peace, but he was not strong enough to look on the beauty of Deirdre knowing she belonged to another man. As soon as he saw her, he went into a jealous rage and ordered his men to attack the sons of Usnach.

But not all of his men were willing to follow their king in this unjust attack, for many were friends of Naois. So the forces of Ireland fought against each other and in the dreadful battle, Naois, Ainle, and Arden were all killed.

A large grave was dug so that the three brothers could be buried together. "Dig it wider," said Deirdre, as she stood beside the open grave and sang a death chant. "Dig it wide, for I must have room beside my beloved."

And as soon as the grave was finished, Deirdre stepped into the tomb, lay down beside her beloved Naois, and died.

the secrets of manhood

In the olden days, a young man was taken into the forest to learn the secrets of manhood before he could be initiated into the adult life of the tribe. During this time he could have nothing at all to do with women.

One day a young girl named Alabe accidentally discovered the young men performing their secret rituals in the sacred forest. Terrified of discovery, she quickly hid behind a bush, but being a woman, she could not resist the desire to see what was going on. One of the young men she saw was so handsome that she immediately fell in love with him.

So instead of running away, she stayed and watched the handsome young man all day. That night as the young men lay down to sleep, Alabe noticed where her favorite was and crept up beside him.

The young man woke up, startled to find a woman by his side. "What are you doing here?" he asked. "Don't you know that it is forbidden for women to be here?"

Alabe just laughed. "I don't easily give up on something I have set my mind on," she boasted. "And now I have set my mind on you." And she began to embrace him passionately.

Soon the young man stopped protesting and began to return her kisses. He became more and more passionate, but suddenly his body shook all over and he fell back stiff and dead. Alabe cried out in alarm, and the other young men came running and caught her.

The chief of the sacred forest called upon

the gods to restore the young man's life. Soon he received a message from the gods and called all of the people of the village together to hear it. He said, "The gods have told me how to save this boy's life. We are to build a huge bonfire and throw a lizard into the middle of it. If someone will rush into the fire and rescue the lizard, he will save the life of the young man."

So the people built a huge bonfire and the chief threw the lizard in. The young man's mother first rushed at the fire, but she could not stand the heat and fell back. The boy's father tried also, but failed.

At last Alabe said, "It is because of me that the young man is dead, so it is up to me to rescue him." With that, she rushed into the center of the fire and brought out the lizard. Then the young man came to life again.

But the people decided that Alabe's evil was too great to be forgiven and threw her back into the center of the still raging flames.

Nature intended women to be our slaves . . . they are our property; we are not theirs. They belong to us, just as a tree that bears fruit belongs to a gardener. What a mad idea to demand equality for women! Women are nothing but machines for producing children.

NAPOLEON BONAPARTE

Believe me, it would have been better far if men could have thought up some other way of producing children, and done away with woman; then no evil would ever have come to men.

JASON, IN EURIPEDES', MEDEA
Translated by Frederick Prokosh

Hidden in the rocks of the Rhine, the Lorelei dangled her locks and lured sailors to their death.

In Greece, the Sirens sang their haunting song which none could resist and which led all who heard it to their death.

In popular myths of all cultures, woman is the temptress who is irresistible and who is both the highest prize and the ultimate destruction of man.

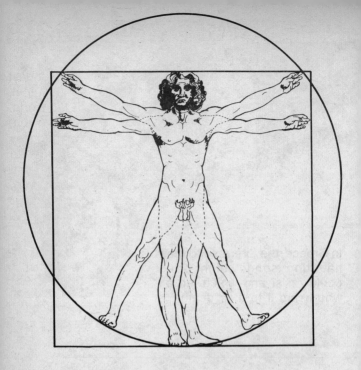

To no form of religion is woman indebted for one impulse of freedom, as all alike have taught her inferiority and subjection.
                    ELIZABETH CADY STANTON

savitri and death

Savitri was the only child of one of the kindest kings of India, and she was the most beautiful, charming, and intelligent woman in the world. In fact, she was so wonderful that all of the eligible men were sure she was a goddess incarnate and would not dare to ask her to marry them. After searching the whole kingdom for a husband for her, the king said to Savitri, "I guess you will have to find a husband for yourself." So he gave her servants and supplies and sent her into the world to find a husband.

Some time later, she returned blushing and smiling. "I have found the man," she said. "He is not rich and powerful, but he is good and kind. He lives in a forest where he cares for his old, blind father. His name is Satyavan."

The sage Narada then came forward. "You have made a good choice, Savitri," he said. "Satyavan is a fine man and his father is really a king whose eyesight and kingdom have been stolen by enemies. But I have very bad news for you. Satyavan is destined to die exactly a year from this day."

Savitri started to cry, but then pulled herself up proudly. "I would rather marry Satyavan for a year than any other man for eternity."

"Perhaps, then, there is hope," said Narada, smiling. "Love like that may be able to conquer death."

Savitri and Satyavan were married and lived happily for a year. But all of this time Savitri prayed and fasted without telling her husband or her in-laws her purpose. At last the day when Satyavan was to die arrived, and Savitri insisted on going with him into the forest. Satyavan

would never deny his beloved wife anything
and was more than glad to have her company.
Suddenly as they were walking through the
forest Satyavan fell down in a faint. Savitri held
his head in her lap and began to pray again.
She seemed to sense a strange presence near
her, and concentrating all of her powers, discovered the form of Yama, the god of death.
She watched as Yama extracted Satyavan's
soul, put it in his noose, and started off for
the land of death. Then she got up and followed
him.

Yama discovered her coming a short distance behind him and said, "Don't try to follow
me. Go back and give your husband's body
a good burial."

96

"I cannot leave my husband," said Savitri. "And I do not believe that that cold body back there is really him. Since you have the real part of my husband, I must follow you, for all my life I have been taught that a wife should follow her husband."

"You are very wise," replied Yama. "I will grant you any wish except the life of your husband."

"If you would, please, give my father-in-law back his sight," Savitri replied, but she did not stop following Yama.

"I thought I told you to go back," Yama said.

"I am sorry," said Savitri, "but I have been taught that one should spend all the time one can in good company, and I perceive that your company is the finest there is."

Yama was very pleased by this, for usually mortals were afraid of him and could not see his good qualities. So he offered Savitri another wish.

"It would make me very happy if my father could have a son, for I am his only child," she replied.

"Granted," replied Yama. "In fact, he shall have a hundred sons. And now you really must go back." But Savitri kept on following him.

"There is so much I can learn from you," she pleaded. "Why should I return to ordinary mortals when your company is so much better?" Yama was so pleased by this that he offered Savitri still another boon, as long as she did not ask for the life of her husband.

"Well, I guess I would like to have a hundred sons for myself," she replied.

"You certainly shall have them," said Yama. "And now will you please go back? You are certainly the most faithful wife I have ever met."

"You are right," said Savitri. "I am a faithful

wife and I will never have anything to do with any man except my husband. So I must ask you one more question. If you carry off my husband in death, how will I ever have the hundred sons you have promised me?"

"You win," said Yama as he loosened his noose from around the soul of Satyavan. "Never before have I returned a life to the land of the living, but never before have I met a woman like you. Take your husband and live with him happily."

tam and the king

Once upon a time there was a widower who had one daughter named Tam. After many years of mourning, he married again and soon his new wife had a daughter named Cam. The new wife loved her own daughter and hated Tam because she was much more beautiful than Cam, so she made her stepdaughter work all day in the kitchen.

One day the mother sent the two girls to the stream to fish. Tam worked hard all day and by evening had a basket full of nice fish, but Cam played in the flowers and did not catch a single one.

When it was time to return home, Cam pointed to Tam and laughed. "Look how ugly you are! Your hair is all dirty and stringy. Why don't you ever wash it?"

Tam looked at her reflection in the stream, and sure enough, she had become dirty and ugly. So she bent her hair to the stream to wash it, and Cam picked up her sister's basket of fish and went home.

When Tam finished washing her hair and looked for her basket, it was gone, and poor Tam began to cry because she knew her stepmother would beat her. But suddenly the goddess of mercy appeared and said, "Don't cry, Tam. Your bad luck will soon be over and the rest of your life will be very happy."

Then the goddess disappeared and Tam found a beautiful golden carp lying where her basket of fish had been. Tam couldn't bear to kill the beautiful fish, so she took it home and hid it in a well. Every day she would sneak out of the kitchen and feed it.

It did not take her stepmother long to discover the fish, and one day when Tam was gone, the stepmother caught the carp, killed it, and ate it.

When Tam returned, she began to cry. Again the goddess of mercy appeared. This time she told Tam to find the bones of the fish and bury them beneath her sleeping mat. Then, whenever she needed anything she could ask the fish. Tam did what the goddess told her.

Soon it was time for the Mid-Autumn Festival and for several days before it, Tam crept to her bed and asked the bones for a new dress, a gold chain, and some new shoes. All of them appeared, and Tam was sure that she would look fine for the big festival. But that morning, her stepmother brought three big baskets of mixed beans and ordered Tam to sort them out. Then she and Cam set off for the festival in the finest clothes they had.

Poor Tam began crying again, and for the

third time, the goddess appeared. She brought with her a flock of ricebirds, who quickly sorted the beans, and a willow wand which she waved over Tam, creating a beautiful blue and silver robe and a pair of brocade slippers.

Off Tam rushed to the festival, where she attracted the attention of everyone, including her stepmother. When Tam saw her stepmother looking at her with an evil stare, she became so frightened that she fled from the festival and returned home. But on the way, she lost one of her brocade slippers and a soldier of the king picked it up and took it to his master.

"This is the finest piece of work I have ever seen," said the king. "Send a message through all of the kingdom that the owner of this slipper should appear before me." The messengers went through the whole kingdom and many ladies claimed the slipper, but none could fit it. At last the messenger came to Tam's house, and, before the astonished eyes of her step-mother and Cam, she appeared in her silver and blue robe, wearing the other brocade slipper.

The messenger took Tam to the court where the king fell in love with her and married her. The cruel stepmother and Cam, however, were so jealous of Tam that they both burst their blood vessels and died!

"Let his name be Tristan, for his birth is sad," breathed Isabella as she lay dying in childbirth in a lonely forest. The queen's squire knelt with her until she died and then took the sad child with him to try to find its father who had been enchanted by a fairy. But Tristan was not destined to find his father, and the squire finally fled with him to France where he grew up. When he came of age the squire took him to the home of his uncle, King Mark of Cornwall.

Things were not going well in Cornwall when Tristan arrived. Sir Moraunt of Ireland had come to the court to demand tribute of King Mark. The knights of Cornwall were well known for cowardice, and apparently deserved their reputation, for no one wished to fight the Irish knight. Finally Tristan begged King Mark to knight him so he could challenge Moraunt.

King Mark was reluctant to do so, but Tristan insisted and as soon as he was knighted met Sir Moraunt in combat. Tristan cut Sir Moraunt's head open, leaving a portion of his sword in the wound. Sir Moraunt quickly returned to his own country where he soon died.

But Tristan was so severely wounded that the doctors of Cornwall could do nothing to help him. At last he decided to sail to England where he had heard that there were skillful surgeons. On the way, he was blown off course and instead landed in Ireland. This was misfortune indeed, for it was the country of Sir Moraunt, whom he had killed, and Sir Moraunt was the brother of the queen. So Tristan decided to conceal his name and called himself Tantris. Thus disguised, he paid a visit to the king's castle.

tristan and isolde

Isolde, the daughter of the king, was skillful with herbs and soon succeeded in curing Tristan. About the time that he was beginning to recover, a great tournament was held and a Saracen knight named Palamedes was winning all of the honors. Tristan noticed that Palamedes seemed to be in love with Isolde, and immediately he became aware of his own great love for her. So he joined the tournament and beat Palamedes.

As soon as he brought his armor out, however, a handmaiden of the queen happened to see his sword and noticed that a piece of it was broken off the same shape as the piece of sword found in the head of Sir Moraunt. The queen demanded vengeance against Tristan, but the king, realizing that Tristan had killed Sir Moraunt in a fair fight, only banished him.

Tristan returned home to King Mark and recounted his adventures, including a marvelous description of the fair Isolde, which so impressed the king that he asked Tristan to go back to Ireland in his behalf and ask for Isolde's hand in marriage.

Tristan could not refuse the king's request, so he set sail again for Ireland, even though he had been warned never to return. He was, obviously, a rather poor seaman, for this time he landed up in England. But it was a fortunate mistake, for the king of Ireland was at that very moment at Camelot pleading for his life. He had been accused of treason and could clear himself of the charges only by meeting one of Arthur's knights in combat. But he had no champion since Sir Moraunt was dead and he was not young enough to fight for himself. So when Tristan offered to fight for him, the old king eagerly agreed and promised him whatever gift he wanted.

Tristan, of course, won the fight and returned with the king to claim Isolde, but not for himself. The queen readily forgave Tristan for killing her brother when she heard that he had saved her husband's life. But she was disturbed by Tristan's request that Isolde marry King Mark, for she knew that Isolde loved Tristan. So she called Isolde's maid, Brengwain, and gave her a love potion which she was to give Isolde and King Mark on the day of their marriage.

But Brengwain was rather careless and left the bottle lying in Isolde's cabin. Tristan and Isolde were sitting together in her cabin and became thirsty. Seeing the bottle lying there, they drank it and immediately fell so deeply in love that there was no escape. Even the power of the love potion could not make Tristan break his word to his uncle, so King Mark and Isolde were married. The king was delighted with his bride, but it did not take him long to become jealous of his nephew.

One day when Tristan was away, a strange knight appeared at the court with a very unusual harp. King Mark was delighted by the harp and asked the stranger to play for him. The stranger said that he would play only if King Mark would grant him a boon. The king agreed, and as soon as the knight, who happened to be Sir Palamedes, had finished, he asked for Isolde as his boon.

The king could not break his word, so he sent Isolde with Palamedes. However, when Tristan returned he immediately set out after Sir Palamedes and challenged him to fight. Isolde refused to let them fight and told Palamedes that if he loved her he should leave immediately.

Tristan stayed hidden with Isolde for a week, but finally returned her to King Mark. But it was not long before the situation at court again became unbearable. At last King Mark caught Tristan and Isolde together and banished Tristan from the kingdom.

Tristan, in despair, returned to England where he became one of the most renowned knights of the Round Table, and eventually, after years of bravery, was offered the hand of the princess of Brittany, who was also named Isolde. Realizing that he was getting old and had no hopes of ever attaining his beloved Isolde, he finally married the girl. Soon the country was in danger again, and in the battle Tristan was seriously wounded.

His wife Isolde tended his wound as best she could, but finally she realized that her skill was not enough. At last, Tristan called his wife to him and told her that he believed that Isolde of Cornwall could cure him and spoke of the time before when she had cured him in Ireland.

So his loving wife sent a ship to Cornwall, and Tristan instructed the ship to raise a white sail if Isolde were coming, but a black sail if she refused. For weeks they waited, and Tristan did his best to hold on to his strength.

But meanwhile his wife began to learn the story of Isolde of Cornwall and realized that she did not want her to cure her husband. When the sail was finally sighted on the horizon, in a fit of jealousy she sent the message that the sail was black.

At these words Tristan gave up hope and died. Shortly afterwards Isolde herself arrived and, finding Tristan dead, she, too, died, holding his body in her arms.

the woman who

There was once a Zuñi maiden who was very poor, for all of her brothers had been killed in the war and she lived with her aged mother and father. Many men had asked her to marry them, but she refused because she did not want to get married.

Since there was no man in the house, there was no meat for the family to eat. The young girl planted beans, pumpkins, squash, and corn, but she and her parents were hungry for meat. She watched enviously as the young men all went out to hunt rabbits and came back with a large string of them.

One day she made an announcement to her parents. "Mother and Father, I am tired of sitting here with no meat. There is no reason why women can't hunt rabbits as well as men can. So tomorrow I am going out to hunt."

Both her parents tried to dissuade her. They were sure she would be lost in the snow. But finally her father was convinced that he could not change her mind and decided to help her. He found the hunting sticks that had belonged to her dead brothers as well as their deerskin boots.

The next morning the girl started off. She had very good luck and by afternoon she found four rabbits. After she killed each of them she raised them reverently and breathed from their noses their expiring breath. She was so busy that she did not notice a snowstorm blowing up. Soon the snow had covered her trail and she did not know which way to go.

wanted to be a hunter

Darkness began to descend and the girl looked for a place to spend the night. At last she found a sheltered place among some rocks and climbed to it. When she got there she found that there was a cave, and best of all, there were still some warm coals left from the last passerby. So the maiden thankfully built the fire back up and soon she was quite comfortable.

But suddenly, as she was sitting there, she heard a horrible rattling noise coming up the slopes. It was the cannibal demon who had seen her fire and had come looking for someone to eat.

The girl crouched in the back of the little cave as the demon came closer and closer. But when he reached the mouth of the cave, he could not get in, for he was too big.

So he tried to trick the girl and called in a gentle voice, "I am cold and hungry. Please come out and bring me something to eat."

"I don't have anything," said the girl, frightened.

"Throw me a rabbit," bellowed the monster—forgetting to be gentle.

The girl obeyed, and the monster continued demanding rabbits until she had no more. Then he demanded her deerskin boots, and devoured them as rapidly as he had eaten the rabbits.

Still the monster made demands and the poor girl was forced to throw him her blanket and even her dress. Then when she had nothing else to throw him, the monster tried again to

107

squeeze into the cave to get the girl.

But now he was even fatter, so he picked up his ax and began pounding the rock around the cave to make the entrance bigger. The poor girl huddled in the corner, not knowing what to do.

The sounds of the demon's ax reached the ears of two gods who were sitting at their home. They immediately understood what had happened, so they picked up their weapons and went to save the girl. Just as the demon was about to enter the cave, they reached him and hit him over the head with their war clubs. They cut open his stomach and took out the girl's clothes and the rabbits.

Then they took the girl her clothes and rabbits and counseled her. "It is better for a woman to follow the normal work for women and not try to do a man's work. Marriage is a very good thing for a woman. You should get married and let your husband do the hunting."

Then the two gods gave the girl a great load of rabbits and took her back to her home. All of the village rejoiced that she was safe and were amazed by the number of rabbits she had.

That very night one of the young men again came to ask her to marry him . . . and this time she gladly agreed. "I have discovered," she said, "that the best way for a woman to provide her family with lots of meat is to marry a husband who can do her hunting for her."

three foolish men

There was once a young man whose parents died and left him a hundred cattle. He was lonely after the death of his parents, so he decided to get married. He went to his neighbors and asked them to help him find a wife.

Soon one of the neighbors came to tell him that he had found the most beautiful girl in the country for him to marry. "The girl is very good and wise and beautiful, and her father is very wealthy," he said. "Her father owns six thousand cattle."

The young man became very excited when he heard about this girl. But then he asked, "How much is the bride price?"

"The father wants a hundred cattle," was the reply.

"A hundred cattle! That is all I have. How will we be able to live?" replied the young man.

"Well, make up your mind. I have to take an answer to the father soon," said the neighbor.

The young man thought, "I cannot live without this girl." So he said, "Go and tell the father that I want to marry his daughter."

So the two were married. But after they returned home, they quickly ran out of food, and the young man had to herd cattle for a neighbor to get anything to eat. What he got was not very much for a young lady who was used to eating well and living in style.

One day as the young wife was sitting outside the house, a strange man came by and was struck by her beauty. He decided to try to seduce her and sent a message to her. The young wife told him that she could not make

109

up her mind and he would have to come back later.

Several months later, the girl's father came to visit. She was very upset because she did not have anything to feed him. But on that same day, the seducer came back. So the young wife told the seducer that she would give in to his requests if he would bring her some meat to cook for her father.

Soon the seducer returned with the meat and the girl went inside to cook it. Her husband returned, and he and her father sat down to eat and have a good time. The seducer was standing outside listening. Soon he became angry and went inside to see what was happening. The young husband, who was hospitable, invited him in.

The young wife then brought in the meat and said, "Eat, you three fools."

"Why do you call us fools?" the three men said all together.

"Well, Father," the girl replied. "You are a fool because you sold something precious for something worthless. You had only one daughter and traded her for a hundred cattle when you already had six thousand."

"You are right," said her father. "I was a fool."

"As for you, husband," she went on. "You inherited only a hundred cattle and you went and spent them all on me, leaving us nothing to eat. You could have married another woman for ten or twenty cows. That is why you were a fool."

"And why am I a fool?" asked the seducer.

"You are the biggest fool of all. You thought you could get for one piece of meat what had been bought for a hundred cattle."

At that, the seducer ran away as fast as he

110

could. Then the father said, "You are a wise daughter. When I get home, I will send your husband three hundred cattle so that you can live in comfort."

hadji and his clever wife

There was once a merchant who had a very clever wife, but he also had a very roving eye. One day a lovely young lady came to his shop and left behind a bag containing twelve grains of wheat. She was so beautiful that Hadji could not stop thinking about her. For days he thought about her, and finally his wife asked him what was the matter. He told her.

"You are silly," his wife said. "She has left you a message in the bag."

"She has?" said Hadji. "What did she say?"

"It is very simple," replied his wife. "She lives in house number twelve by the wheat market."

Hadji rushed off to the wheat market and found the house. He knocked at the door, and sure enough, the lovely young lady came to the door. However, instead of inviting him in, she threw a pail of water out the door and then shut the door.

So Hadji returned home to ask his wife what to do next.

"She is telling you to go around back where there is a stream and meet her there," she replied.

Sure enough, when Hadji returned he found a stream behind her house and the lovely young lady waiting for him.

He also found the police, for Hadji's wife had informed the police as soon as she had told him where to go.

So Hadji and the young lady were carried off to prison on grounds of immoral conduct.

The next morning Hadji's wife went to the

112

prison and asked the jailer to let her give alms to the prisoners. When she arrived in the young lady's cell, she offered to change places with her if the young lady would never again have anything to do with her husband.

Therefore, when Hadji was brought before the judge, he found, not the lovely lady, but his wife, who protested vehemently against being arrested for conversing with her own husband in a garden.

The surprised judge let them go, and Hadji went home amazed at his wife's wisdom. Never again did he try to look at other women.

psyche and eros

Aphrodite, the goddess of love and beauty, came down from Mount Olympus to enjoy the praises of men at one of her many shrines. But she found it empty. Not a single worshipper had come to her altar. For in the town crowds of people were following a beautiful girl named Psyche and strewing flowers in her path as they had once done for Aphrodite.

Aphrodite was furious and returned to heaven in a rage. She called her son Eros, or Cupid as he was known to the Romans, to her and told him to take his bow and arrow and ruin this haughty girl.

"Make her fall in love with the ugliest, most low-class person or beast you can," she ordered.

But when Eros arrived in Psyche's room and saw her, he was so struck by her beauty that he fell in love with her. And instead of shooting his arrow at an ugly, low-born man, he wounded himself with it. Then he disappeared.

For some time after that, Psyche continued living as she had before. But she was beginning to worry about marriage. Both of her older sisters were now married, but no suitors had come for her. They seemed to be afraid of her wonderful beauty.

At last, in despair, her father sent a messenger to ask Apollo's oracle if they had by chance offended some god who would therefore not allow Psyche to be married. The answer from the oracle was strange and horrible. "Psyche is not destined to be the wife of a mortal man. Her husband waits for her on the top of the mountain, and you must take her there at once. He is a monster that neither men nor gods can resist."

Psyche and her family all wept at these words, but they knew better than to disobey the orders of the gods. So Psyche was dressed in wedding garments and taken to the top of the mountain. Her weeping family left her there and Psyche, tired and sorrowful, finally fell asleep.

Zephyr, the gentle wind, lifted her in her sleep and carried her down from the mountain to a castle. When Psyche awoke she was amazed to see the most beautiful palace in the world, surrounded by gardens and fountains. Then she heard a voice coming from an invisible being, "Lady, all that you see before you is yours. We are your servants to do whatever you wish."

Filled with amazement, Psyche walked through the garden and into the house. There were golden pillars and beautiful paintings and statues. When she was hungry, a feast appeared before her, and unseen hands played the lute for her enjoyment.

And that night her husband came to her. He

was gentle and kind, and Psyche loved him even though she never saw him. For he always came after dark and left before the rays of morning sun began to shine.

One night, though, her husband was troubled and worried. "Your sisters are coming to the mountain to look for you tomorrow. And I fear they bring some kind of danger."

"Oh, no," cried Psyche. "They are good and loving, and I have been so sad knowing that they think I am dead. Please let me see them and show them this beautiful castle."

"I am afraid that they will try to make you want to see what I look like, and that can never be," said her husband.

"I love you," said Psyche. "And nothing they could say would make me do anything to jeopardize our happiness."

"All right," replied her husband. "It is against my better judgment, but I will allow them to come here to visit you."

The next day the two sisters arrived and were at first very happy to see their sister alive. But as they wandered through the beautiful castle and ate the delicious food, they became dreadfully jealous.

"And where is your husband?" they asked.

"He is out hunting," replied Psyche.

But it did not take them long to find out that Psyche had actually never seen her husband and had no idea where he went during the day.

"He is the monster that the oracle warned you about!" said the sisters. "He probably is waiting for you to have a child so he can devour you both."

"No, I am sure he is not," said Psyche. But the seeds of doubt had been planted.

"Let me tell you what to do," said the older sister. "Tonight, when he is asleep, take a lamp

116

and a knife. Hold the lamp over his face and look at him. If he is indeed a monster, then plunge the knife into his heart. That way you can escape."

"I could never do that!" cried Psyche.

But that night, when her husband was asleep, Psyche lay awake. At last she could no longer stand the suspense and picked up the lamp and held it over his face. She gasped at the beauty of what she saw. The god of love himself lay there. Overcome, Psyche knelt to kiss him, but as she knelt a drop of oil from the lamp fell on his body. Instantly Eros was awake and realized that Psyche had betrayed him.

Immediately he spread his wings and flew away with these words: "Your only punishment is that I am leaving you forever. Love cannot live with suspicion."

Eros flew back to his mother's house to nurse his wounded heart, and Psyche was left alone in sorrow. In despair she started to drown herself in the river, but the kindly river god stopped her and said, "You are young and beautiful. Do not end your life like this. If you have problems, serve the gods and pray to them for help."

So Psyche went to a temple of Demeter and set to work cleaning and straightening it. Demeter was pleased by the girl's work, but when she heard who she was, she said, "Aphrodite is angry with you, Psyche. I would like to help you, but I cannot make her angry. You must go to Aphrodite herself and offer to serve her. Then perhaps you can win her favor."

So Psyche went to the house of Aphrodite.

"Well, so you have finally decided to come to pay your respects to your in-law," said Aphrodite. "I have heard what a disobedient wife you have been. Let's see if you can be an obedient daughter-in-law."

So Aphrodite set impossible tasks for Psyche to do. First she took her to a storehouse in which all kinds of grains were mixed together. "Separate all of these into the different kinds and make sure you are finished by evening."

But Psyche did not even know where to begin. Fortunately, the ants took pity on her and separated all of the grain for her. Then they disappeared.

When Aphrodite saw that she had succeeded with this task, she was angry and told her to go to a field nearby and gather golden wool from the sheep. The river god helped her and told her to gather the fleece from the brambles the sheep walked through.

When she returned with her arms full of fleece, Aphrodite was even more angry.

"Tomorrow," she said, "you are to take this box to Persephone in the land of the dead and ask for her special beauty treatment."

Psyche did not know of any way to get to the land of the dead except by killing herself, so she climbed a tall tower to jump off. But as she reached the top, she heard a voice pointing out a path to Hades. "Take with you two loaves of bread. Use one loaf to stop the mouth of Cerberus when you enter, and feed him the other loaf when you come out. Do not eat anything you are offered in Hades and do not look into the box before you give it to Aphrodite."

Psyche followed the advice of the voice and overcame all of the dangers of Hades. But as she was returning to Aphrodite with the box, she was overcome with curiosity again and, for the second time in her life, could not withstand the temptation.

"Perhaps if I had this special secret of

beauty," she thought, "I could win back my husband Eros."

Psyche looked into the box. The secret of Persephone's beauty was sleep! And Psyche immediately fell into a deep trance.

But in the meantime, Eros had recovered and decided to forgive his curious wife. So he flew down to her and gathered the sleep from her and returned it to the box. Then he took Psyche and flew before Zeus himself. Eros, indeed, was the "monster neither men nor gods could resist," and Zeus himself had suffered plenty from his arrows. So he was glad to finally see the boy caught in his own trap.

The king of gods, himself, gave Psyche the cup of ambrosia which made her immortal, and she and Eros lived happily forever.

THE TWO SHALL BE ONE FLESH

Male and female, yin and yang, Psyche and Eros, soul and body. The sexes are separate, sometimes opposing each other, sometimes seeking to dominate each other, but always both are necessary for life to continue.

Some mythologies try to show the unity of the two sexes in one androgynous person:

Some interpretations of Genesis claim that since Eve was taken from Adam's body, Adam himself must have originally incorporated both sexes and that the real fall was when the two were separated.

In Greek mythology, Hermes and Aphrodite had a child named Hermaphrodite who had the characteristics of both sexes.

Awonawilona, the chief god of the Zuñis, is at first both male and female and must separate into two parts to begin creation.

Tiresias, the blind seer of the Oedipus story and the *Odyssey*, was both male and female.

Siva and his wife often appear united in a single body in statues. The left half is female and the right side is male. This manifestation is called Ardhanarisha.

cut here

WHAT IS
THE PERFECT MAN?

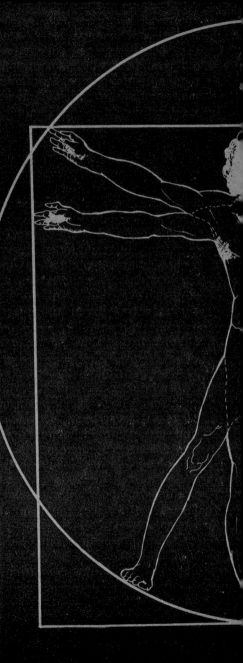

INSIGHTS FROM MYTHOLOGY

For every man who comes into the world there is a way, a Tao, a Blessing Way, that leads from the mysteries before birth to the mysteries beyond death. It is the function of the myths of the hero and the rituals which they instituted to make this way known to ordinary men and to guide them safely upon it. Infancy, childhood, manhood, and old age all bring crises which no man may escape, and at every turn we are all faced by monsters within ourselves and from the outside. At these times of stress, mythology provides symbols, rituals, and models to guide our choices and ease our stresses.

> In dealing with symbols and myths from far away, we are really conversing with ourselves—with a part of ourselves, however, which is as unfamiliar to our conscious being as the interior of the earth to the students of geology. Hence the mythical tradition provides us with a sort of map for exploring and ascertaining contents of our own inner being to which we consciously feel only scantily related.
>
> **HEINRICH ZIMMER**

In our faiths, in our art, in our dreams, and sometimes in our insanity, we wrestle with the universal symbols of our fears and worries. Snakes, monsters, fire, water, and flight for us—as for all mankind—symbolize our subconscious desires and fears and our frightening choices. And we, who have rejected the guidance which our ancestors so carefully worked into their myths and rituals, are often forced to develop our own personal myths on the analyst's couch.

There is much the stories of heroes can teach us about good and evil and how a man can cope with them, about successful psychological development, and about what it means to be human. Listen as the ancient voices answer the question: "Who is the perfect man?"

124

rama

"Who is the perfect man?" asked the sage Valmiki.

And the answer that came to his ears was: "Rama, Rama, Rama, Rama, Rama Rama,

Rama, Rama, Rama, Rama, Rama, Rama.''

So meditating on the holy name of Rama, Valmiki composed the sacred poem, the *Ramayana,* even before Rama himself was born.

Rama was not an ordinary prince, for he was the avatar, or incarnation, of the god Vishnu, come to earth to save the world from the demon Ravana.

But he appeared to be a fairly normal person when he was born the son of King Dasaratha. While he was still quite young, the sage Viswamitra appeared before King Dasaratha and requested that Rama and Lakshmana, one of his brothers, come with him to keep the demons away from the temple where he and other sages were trying to sacrifice.

The king did not want to send his young sons off, but Rama and Lakshmana insisted that they were eager to try their strength, so they followed the sage. The next day as the sages began their sacrifices, the demons again attacked them. But this time Rama and Lakshmana fought them off with their bow and arrow, and the sages could then sacrifice in peace.

While the young men were there, they heard that the Swayamwara of the beautiful daughter of King Janaka was to be held. A Swayamwara was a means by which a lady would choose a husband for herself, and both Rama and Lakshmana decided to try their luck.

Rama was immediately struck by the beauty of Sita and fell in love with her. He was pleased when he discovered that the task she had set for the men to prove themselves was to string a bow which Siva had given to King Janaka. Rama, who was already famous as an archer, easily bent the great bow and claimed Sita for his bride. So the two brothers returned home proudly with Sita.

But good fortune did not await them at home. Kaikeyi, Rama's father's third wife, was jealous of Rama's success and knew that he would soon be appointed heir to the throne. Her own son, Bharata, being younger than Rama and the son of the third wife, had no claim to the throne. But she had a claim on the king. Once she had saved his life on the battlefield and he had promised to grant her two favors. Now she was ready to ask for them.

"Dasaratha," she said one day as he was relaxing in her chamber. "Do you remember the time I saved your life during battle?"

"Of course I remember," replied Dasaratha. "And I also remember that I offered to grant you two boons which you have not yet used."

"I am now ready to ask those boons," replied Kaikeyi. "The first boon is that my son Bharata be named heir to the throne. And the second boon is that Rama be banished from the kingdom for fourteen years."

King Dasaratha wept when he heard her requests. He hated the thought of losing Rama as his heir, but he could not go back on his word. When the king announced that Rama was to be banished, Sita, his wife, insisted on going with him. "A wife's place is with her husband," she said. "And whether his home is a palace or a hovel, she must be beside him."

Rama knew that she was right, and he was glad for her company. His brother Lakshmana also insisted that he be allowed to go with him. So the three of them found a small but comfortable cave in the forest and prepared to stay for fourteen years.

Bharata had been away when all of this happened and knew nothing of his mother's request. When he returned he found that his father had died from grief and that he himself was to be crowned king. He refused to accept the kingdom won so unfairly and set out to find Rama. After months of searching in the forest, he found Rama and said, "I have come to beg forgiveness for what my mother has done and to ask you to return to the city as king."

But Rama replied, "My father made a vow, and it is my duty to fulfill it. I will not return until the fourteen years are up."

When Bharata realized that he could never persuade Rama to return, he asked, "Then give me your sandals that I can take them back and set them upon the throne. They will serve as a reminder that you are the real king and I am

only serving as your regent until you return in fourteen years." Rama complied, and Bharata returned sadly to the capital. Lakshmana, Sita, and Rama remained in the forest living a blissful and idyllic life.

However, their peace did not last long, for the demoness Surpanakha came into the forest one day and saw the two handsome young men. She was determined to marry one of them, but Rama pointed out that he was already married. Lakshmana, even though he was not married, would have nothing to do with her. At last, enraged, Surpanakha attacked Sita, and Lakshmana angrily drew his sword and cut off her nose, ears, and breasts.

Furious, she flew to her brother, the demon Ravana, on his island fortress.

"See how I have been treated," she cried, showing his whole court her mutilated face. "You must avenge me!"

"Who has done this to you?" asked Ravana.

"The brothers Rama and Lakshmana," she replied.

Ravana's court advisers immediately warned him that he must have nothing to do with these two, that Rama was the most powerful archer in the world and seemed to be blessed with supernatural power.

But this challenge only whetted Ravana's appetite.

"Besides," said Surpanakha, "the best way to get revenge would be to steal Rama's wife, Sita. Then he would die of a broken heart. And Sita would be a good addition to your collection of beautiful young maidens."

So Ravana sent one of his men disguised as a golden deer that grazed close by the cave of Rama and Sita.

Looking out the opening of the cave, Sita

129

was delighted by the beautiful animal and asked Rama to get it for her.

"I am afraid that there is something magic about it," Rama replied.

"Oh, please," begged Sita. "It is the most beautiful thing I have seen since we left the city."

Realizing how much Sita had suffered by following him into exile, Rama agreed. "All right, if it is a real deer I will bring it to you alive. If it is an evil spirit, I can kill it and bring you the hide."

Swiftly Rama started after the deer, but it darted away easily, staying far in front of him. For several hours he followed the deer that teasingly stayed just in sight but too far away for him to catch. As they came to a ridge on a strange mountain, Rama realized how far he had traveled, and suddenly he knew that the strange deer must be a trick to lure him away from Sita. Very worried, he quickly drew an arrow and shot the mysterious deer straight through the heart. But with its dying breath, the deer cried loudly, "Help, Lakshmana! I am dying! Save me!"

Back in their cave, Lakshmana heard what he thought was his brother's cry for help and, forgetting his duty to protect Sita, rushed toward the sound of the cry.

As soon as he was gone, the demon Ravana, in the form of a hermit, appeared to Sita and forced her to show him hospitality by going into the cave to fix him something to eat. As soon as she was inside he assumed his horrible form, a ten-headed demon, and imprisoned her. Sita screamed in terror, but he put one of his thousand hands over her mouth, and with another grabbed her hair and dragged her off in his chariot.

Hearing Sita's scream, Rama and Lakshmana rushed back to their home, but they could find no trace of her. They knew that she must have been carried off by a terrible demon but had no idea where to begin looking. As the two brothers were still searching their cave in despair, a huge vulture fell from the sky to their feet. Rama rushed to the giant bird and saw that he had been wounded in several spots and was near to death.

"Sita has been captured by Ravana," the great bird gasped. "I tried to rescue her but failed. He has imprisoned her on his island." As soon as he had whispered these words, the vulture died. Rama felt a strange recognition of this bird, but he could not yet know that he was an incarnation of the god Vishnu and the vulture was an incarnation of his sacred mount, Garuda.

Meanwhile, Ravana had carried Sita to his island fortress where he put her in his harem. He planned to make her another of his wives, but she refused to have anything to do with him, even when he threatened to kill and eat her if she would not yield to him. Finally he told her she had a year to make up her mind and then she must either marry him or die.

Rama and Lakshmana despaired of ever rescuing Sita, for they had discovered that Ravana was the most powerful of all the demons and had dared to threaten the gods themselves. He seemed almost invincible, for he had the promise of Indra that he could not be killed by any god.

While Rama and Lakshmana were traveling toward Ravana's island and trying to think up a plan to attack him, they found a monkey who was in distress. He was the king of monkeys and had been forced out of his kingdom. Rama and Lakshmana, deciding that his cause was just, helped him to regain his throne, and the grateful monkey king offered his army and his general Hanuman to Rama to assist him in his struggle.

Hanuman, who had magical powers, proved a very valuable ally. First he went on a spy mission to Ravana's home where he found Sita weeping in a garden. Comforting her, he told her of Rama's plans. Then he mischievously began destroying Ravana's city—tearing up trees, pulling down buildings, and knocking over the towers. The furious Ravana sent his whole army after him, but the agile monkey mocked them from the tops of trees and towers as he continued his destruction. At last, however, he was caught, and Ravana decreed that his soldiers should burn him by tying oily rags to his tail.

Hanuman pretended to be terrified by this edict and moaned and wailed as the rags were tied and lighted. But then he grew to a giant size and dashed to the sea, setting the whole city on fire with his burning tail as he went.

When Hanuman returned from his spy mission, Rama and the rest of the monkeys marched to the seashore across from Ravana's island.

"Part for us, so we can cross to Ravana's island," Rama cried to the ocean. But the ocean replied, "We cannot disobey the laws of nature for you. You must use other means. If you will build a causeway, though, we will be careful not to disturb it."

So Rama and the monkeys built a great causeway to Ravana's island. As Ravana and his men watched their progress, his advisers urged the great demon to return Sita so they would not all be killed. But he would not listen

133

to them. His pride was so great that he felt he was invincible. Certainly he was not afraid of a few men and an army of monkeys!

At last Rama and his monkey army reached Ravana's city, and a great battle raged for many days. At last all of the demons except Ravana were killed, and Rama engaged him in single combat. Ravana, who had not bothered to ask Indra to make him invincible against mere men, was certainly a powerful adversary. He had ten heads, and when one was cut off, another grew in its place. But Rama also had a powerful weapon, the Astra, the sacred weapon of Brahma, and when he threw it, it landed in Ravana's heart and killed him.

Finally Sita was freed and joyfully rushed into Rama's arms. But Rama held her at arm's length.

"You have been defiled by another man," said Rama sadly. "I can no longer consider you my wife."

Sita was stunned. "But Rama," she pled. "He never came near me."

Rama was adamant. "I will continue to take care of you, but I will never touch you again," he said and turned to walk away.

"Wait!" Sita cried and her voice was terrible. "Lakshmana," she ordered, "bring wood and build a fire. I call on the gods to prove my innocence!"

A huge fire was built right in the middle of the battlefield and when the flames were towering high above the heads of the men, Sita threw herself on it. Immediately the flames formed themselves into the shape of a god, lifted Sita from the ground, and set her down in front of Rama.

Rama embraced her joyfully, for the gods had now shown that he could accept her without damaging his self-respect. So Rama and Sita and Lakshmana returned to their home, where Bharata still waited with Rama's sandals on the throne. Amid the rejoicing of all the people, Rama assumed the throne and ruled well for many years.

But the couple's troubles were still not over. After several years rumors began to fly around the capital that Sita had been unfaithful with Ravana. Since no one there had seen Sita's trial by fire except Rama and Lakshmana, there was no one who could vindicate her, and at last Rama decided to send her into exile.

Sita started off on her journey, thinking that she would visit the cave where she and Rama had been in exile together so many years before. But on the way she came to the ashram of the sage Valmiki, who had all this time been composing a great poem, *The Ramayana,* not yet knowing whether his hero had even been born. He greeted Sita very warmly and begged her to stay there. Sita was very glad to find a kind home, for she was pregnant and in a few months bore twin boys, Kusa and Lava.

As the boys grew up, Valmiki taught them *The Ramayana,* which he was still composing. At last a great ceremony was held in Rama's kingdom, and Valmiki sent Kusa and Lava, who had now learned the whole poem, to participate in it. While the ceremony was going on, the two voices were suddenly heard reciting the great poem. Rama and all of his men were thrilled by it and called the boys to them. For days and days the whole city sat spellbound listening to the tremendous epic, and when it was finished they all sat in silence.

At last Rama asked, "Who are you and where did you learn this poem?"

"Our mother is Sita, and our father is a great

135

king, but we do not know him," the boys replied.

Then Rama wept and gathered them to him. "Go get Sita and bring her to me," he begged Lakshmana. "I want her here whatever the rumors may say."

So Sita again was returned to Rama, but this time she refused to accept a man who had twice accused her of unfaithfulness.

"Mother Earth," she cried. "If I have been pure, take me unto yourself!" And before the startled eyes of the crowd, the earth opened and Sita disappeared into it.

Rama went mad with rage and despair. He cried to the earth to give him back his wife. His friends feared that he would take his own life. But suddenly Brahma himself appeared to him.

"Have you become so wrapped up in the world of illusion that you have forgotten who you are? You are the great Lord Vishnu and this body you are in is only a temporary form you assumed in order to destroy Ravana. This woman you called Sita was an incarnation of your eternal wife Lakshmi and she awaits you in your heavenly home."

Rama was once again at peace, and a short time afterward he walked into the River Sarayu and disappeared from the earth to the heavens where as Vishnu he continues to watch over the world and wait for another time when he must come to earth again to save it from destruction.

"Tell me who I am," begged a young man of Troezan in southern Greece.

"I can't," said his mother. "Your father made me promise that I would never tell you his name until you prove yourself worthy to be his son. He left a task for you." And with that she got up and led the boy into the forest to a huge stone.

"Under this stone," she said, "are your father's gifts to you. If you can lift the stone, you will be his heir. If not, you must stay with me."

The young man strained at the huge stone and finally, with almost superhuman effort, lifted it. Under the stone was a finely made sword with insignia unfamiliar to him. His mother smiled proudly and told him her long-kept secret.

"Your father is Aegeus, the king of Athens. We were married in secret and he left before you were born. He was afraid to take us with him because he had so many enemies who wanted the throne, and he did not want you to come to Athens unless you were strong enough to hold the throne yourself."

So Theseus set off for Athens, the city he would rule for so many years. But he was not satisfied to go to his father with his only achievement the lifting of a stone, so he decided to go on his trip by land instead of by sea. A land journey through that part of Greece was almost unheard of because all of the roads were infested by sadistic robbers. The worst of these was Procrustes who tortured everyone he captured by laying them out on an iron bed

Aegean Sea (from Aegeus, Greek king, father of Theseus): an arm of the Mediterranean Sea east of Greece

theseus

138

and either cutting or stretching them to fit. Theseus caught the cruel old cutthroat and killed him on his own bed. By the time Theseus reached Athens, he had killed several such characters and had made the road to Athens safe for travelers, at least temporarily.

Aegeus, in the meantime, had married the sorceress Medea, who had fled to him after being thrown out by her former husband, Jason. Through her magic arts she knew that Theseus was the heir to the throne and plotted his death. She told Aegeus that she had seen signs that Theseus was an enemy coming to kill him and urged him to give the young man a cup of poisoned wine which she would prepare.

That night at the banquet, Aegeus called the newly arrived young man to him and offered him the cup. Theseus raised his arm to drink, but suddenly Aegeus struck it out of his hand. Theseus' cloak had fallen back and Aegeus could see his sword at his side.

"Where is Medea?" he cried in anger. But Medea was already running through the courtyard and escaped from her evil deeds in a magic chariot.

Aegeus begged his son's forgiveness and immediately proclaimed him to Athens as his heir.

But Aegeus was no longer as powerful as he had once been. Shortly after Theseus arrived in the city, a ship from Crete came to collect the annual tribute of six young men and six maidens who were to be devoured by a monster called Minotaur.

This Minotaur was half bull, half man, and according to legend was the son of the queen herself and a sacred bull. The king had been supposed to sacrifice the bull to Poseidon, but

Procrustean (from Procrustes, a villain in Greek mythology who tortured people by stretching or cutting them to make them fit his bed): marked by ruthless disregard for individual differences

Poor woman — poor Sita, Ariadne, and Medea — who leaves her father's house and uses her magic arts to help the hero — who then rejects her and deserts her. Isn't it possible for the hero and his wife to remain together happily?

had refused. So Poseidon made the queen fall in love with the bull, and the Minotaur was the result. To hide this horrible monster, the king had summoned the most clever inventor of the day, Daedalus, who had built the Labyrinth, a huge maze from which it was impossible to escape. Once each year six men and six maidens were fed to the monster to appease him.

"How can you call yourself a king when you accept this kind of treatment?" Theseus asked his father.

"We have no choice," the old king replied sadly. "Several years ago a Cretan prince was killed in Athens. This is our punishment. Crete is such a powerful enemy that we feel lucky they did not destroy our whole city."

Theseus pleaded in vain for his father to resist the tribute, but without success. At last he said, "All right, if twelve of our subjects must go to feed this monster, I will be one of them. But I am not going to be eaten. I am going to kill the Minotaur!"

Aegeus could not dissuade Theseus from his decision, and when the ship sailed for Crete, Theseus was one of the young men. The new Athenian victims were brought before the court of the king of Crete and everyone knew that the handsomest was the prince of Athens. Ariadne, the king's daughter, was so impressed with Theseus that she fell in love with him and resolved to rescue him.

She went to Daedalus secretly and asked him how a person could escape from the Labyrinth. He gave her a ball of thread and told her that a person could return from the Labyrinth by

140

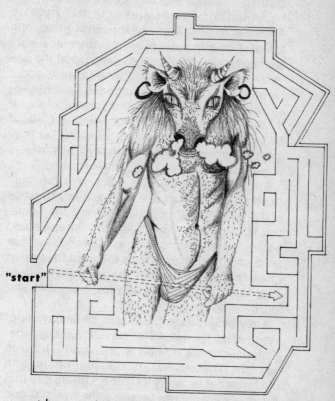

"start"

What is the monster, half man, half beast that
waits to destroy the hero? Is it perhaps the animal
within his own nature?

unrolling the thread as he went in and following it back out.

Then Ariadne slipped into the room where the Athenians were imprisoned. She told the startled Theseus that she could rescue him if he would marry her and take her back to Athens with him. Theseus quickly agreed, and the next morning as the twelve Athenians were led into the Labyrinth, Theseus carried the ball of thread. As soon as the guards were gone, he began to unroll it. Through the twisted passageway they walked together, always alert, for they did not know what turn or twist would reveal the hideous monster. Suddenly, as they stepped down a short stairway, they saw a huge shape lying asleep on the ground.

Theseus leaped on his back and the bull-headed monster awoke with a roar. Theseus and the Minotaur wrestled fiercely for hours, but at last the Athenian gained a stranglehold about the monster's neck and killed him. Theseus and his friends quickly followed the thread back to the entrance of the Labyrinth. There they found Ariadne waiting for them, and she led them to their ship.

They sailed from Crete and a few days later stopped at the island of Naxos. Exactly what happened there no one is quite certain. Some say that Theseus was simply ungrateful and did not want to marry Ariadne. Others say that Ariadne went ashore because she was sick and a wind blew Theseus' ship away. Whatever the reason, Thesus left Ariadne behind on the island and sailed for Athens. Ariadne, of course, was furious, but things turned out well for her, because the god Dionysus found her there and married her.

Theseus, however, was plagued by bad luck with women. After he returned to Athens and became king, he led an expedition against the Amazons, a fierce group of women warriors from Asia Minor who worshipped Artemis. During the battle, Theseus fell in love with and captured the queen of the Amazons, Hippolyta. He carried her back to his home where she had a son named Hippolytus. But the Amazons were unwilling to lose their queen and marched against Theseus, and in the battle, Hippolyta was killed. Next, Theseus and his friend Pirithous of Thessaly, whose wife had also died, decided they would choose no mere mortal women for their next wives but would both marry daughters of Zeus. Theseus was somewhat modest and only went after a little girl named Helen, who later became known as Helen of Troy. But her two brothers, Castor and Polydeuces, rescued her.

Pirithoüs, however, was far bolder and decided that he would capture none other than Persephone, the wife of Hades, god of the underworld. Taking Theseus with him, Pirithoüs brazenly went to the underworld. Hades, who of course knew of their plot all along, cordially welcomed them and invited them to sit down and talk with him. They both sat down, and there they stayed, for they had sat on the rock of forgetfulness, which makes anyone sitting on it forget all he ever knew and keeps him a prisoner forever. Fortunately Theseus had a cousin—Hercules—who was even bolder than he was. Sometime later Hercules came to the underworld on an errand, and when he saw Theseus sitting there, he picked him right up off the rock and took him back to the land of the living.

By this time Theseus must have been rather old, but he still decided to marry again. This time he chose Phaedra, the daughter of the king of Crete who had tried to feed him to the Minotaur, and the sister of Ariadne whom he had deserted at Naxos. Hardly an auspicious choice, for Phaedra brought as much evil with her as might have been predicted.

By the time Phaedra came to Athens, Theseus' son Hippolytus was grown and was apparently a very handsome young man. But following the tradition of his mother's people, the Amazons, he devoted his life to the chaste goddess Artemis and refused to have anything to do with women. Aphrodite was quite insulted by this insolent young man and she caused Phaedra to fall in love with him.

Unable to control her passionate love for Hippolytus, Phaedra called him to come to her chamber. She made him swear before his goddess Artemis that he would never reveal to anyone what she was about to tell him, and Hippolytus, seeing her distress and anxious to be helpful, agreed.

Then Phaedra told Hippolytus that she was madly in love with him and she tried to kiss him. Hippolytus flung her from him in horror and fled from her room.

In despair at her disgrace and rejection, Phaedra hanged herself, leaving a note saying that Hippolytus had raped her. Theseus himself found her body. When he found her note, he seemed to go mad. He called Hippolytus before him and banished him from the city. As the boy left, Theseus cursed him and called on Poseidon to punish him.

Unfortunately, Poseidon obeyed his worshipper's plea. Hippolytus hitched up his chariot and drove furiously down the rocky seacoast away from his father. As the chariot rounded a steep turn, a giant sea monster rose out of the sea and the terrified horses plunged over the side of the cliff. The chariot shattered on the rocks and Hippolytus' mangled body was caught inside.

Artemis watched the death of her beloved follower helplessly. She knew she could not interfere with fate, but she helped her worshipper all she could. She sent a fisherman to find the still-breathing body and take it back to his father, and she herself appeared to Theseus.

"You have done a great wrong in acting so hastily," she told him sadly. "Your son was innocent. It was Phaedra who tried to seduce him."

Just then the fisherman appeared with Hippolytus, who lived only long enough to hear his father's words. "If only I could die for you!" Theseus cried in anguish, but against death the hero had no power.

What is the monster, half man, half beast, which irresistibly draws each of us into his presence where we behold him with a mixture of delight and horror?

MONSTERS

Every Saturday morning the great American monster ritual begins as millions of children rush to their television sets for the morning cartoons. They watch caricatures of space men, wizards, foxes, gorillas, and papier-mâché dinosaurs bammed, bopped, and chased off cliffs by Mighty Mouse, Bugs Bunny, Batman, and other of our noble cultural heroes. That night their more mature parents and older siblings cling to each other in horror and delight through the Creature Features, the Late Creature Features, and the Late-Late Creature Features, enjoying such favorites as Frankenstein, Dracula, the Mummy, and King Kong.

Ogres, banshees, goblins, ghosts, witches, and vampires populate man's imagination as thoroughly as wolves, bears, and snakes populate his land. Why do men almost universally invent monsters? What do they signify? Can they possibly serve any useful purpose?

148

Sometimes our pictures of monsters are created out of the mysterious or evil forces which we recognize within ourselves. An array of creatures who were half man, half beast roamed the Greek forests. Centaurs, who were half man, half horse, were a quarrelsome, drunken lot, but one of their number, Chiron, had great wisdom and was the teacher of Achilles. The satyrs, also known as fauns and sylvans, were half goat and half human. Even more frequently drunk than the centaurs, they were followers of Dionysus and delighted in his frenzied rituals. Both species could be seen as personifying the fears men have of their animal-inherited nature which inclines them to anger and madness.

Even more obviously a symbol of our inner forces, elves are small, tricky beings whose activities range from friendly pranks to stealing cattle and children. It was believed that nightmares were caused by elves sitting on a person's chest; the German word for nightmare is derived from their name.

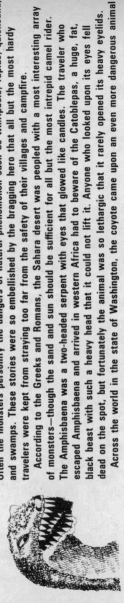

Traveling into the unknown was a deed that only the hero has dared to do, and usually he has returned with tales of strange and fearsome beasts to make sure that no one follows in his path. Often the monsters personify the dangers of natural phenomenon such as whirlpools, rapids, quicksand, and swamps. These stories were so embellished by the bragging hero that all but the most hardy travelers were kept from straying too far from the safety of their villages and campfire.

According to the Greeks and Romans, the Sahara desert was peopled with a most interesting array of monsters—though the sand and sun should be sufficient for all but the most intrepid camel rider. The Amphisbaena was a two-headed serpent with eyes that glowed like candles. The traveler who escaped Amphisbaena and arrived in western Africa had to beware of the Catoblepas, a huge, fat, black beast with such a heavy head that it could not lift it. Anyone who looked upon its eyes fell dead on the spot, but fortunately the animal was so lethargic that it rarely opened its heavy eyelids.

Across the world in the state of Washington, the coyote came upon an even more dangerous animal

150

in his travels. This beast, the sucking monster, was so huge that the entire valley in which the coyote was traveling was a part of his stomach. The animal's heart, which the coyote cut out, was a range of mountains.

The sea, of course, was peopled by monsters ranging from Leviathan, a whalelike creature, to Remora, a fish that could create a vacuum which would hold a ship becalmed. It is no wonder that Columbus' sailors did not want to venture out into the unknown sea.

Whether they symbolize external or internal dangers, the hero knows that monsters are there to be killed. And once he has slain them, the power that was theirs belongs to him. So Siegfried drank the blood of Fenris, and Perseus took the head of Medusa. For the same reason, many rituals involved taking the head, claws, or antlers of animals which were killed, or drinking their blood. Cannibalism and head-hunting served the same function: of giving the killer the power of his victim. Killing the monster gives supernatural powers to the hero.

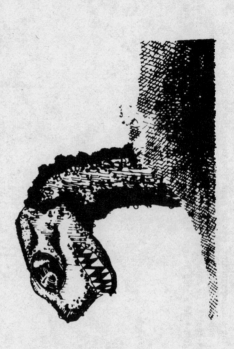

GREEK

Every man's birth is a miracle. The child set adrift or abandoned is a familiar theme in mythology. Moses, Cyrus the Great, Oedipus, King Arthur, Perseus, Theseus, and Krishna were all sent away as infants and grew up in a strange land. Are these myths an attempt to invent a kingly lineage for a man who deserves it? Or do they reflect the universal wish that each of us may someday lift the stone and be proclaimed the child of a king?

perseus

King Acrisius of Argos was an unhappy man, for an oracle had prophesied that he would never have any sons and that the son of his daughter, Danaë, would kill him.

The only way to escape this horrible fate would be to kill Danaë, but Acrisius was not willing to do that. Instead, he built a very tall tower and imprisoned Danaë inside it. There was no way any man could get to her.

This was exactly the kind of challenge that Zeus liked. He changed himself into a shower of gold, and nine months later, Danaë had a son.

For several years she was able to keep the child hidden, but at last her father found him. Still unwilling to shed blood, he put the mother and child in a chest and cast them into the sea. They were rescued by a kind fisherman named Dictys, who took care of the mother and her son, whom she named Perseus.

They eventually came to the attention of the king of the land, Polydectes, who tried to force Danaë to marry him. She refused. But the king thought that she might be more willing if her son were not around to defend her. So he sent Perseus on a mission which he was sure was doomed to failure: he asked Perseus to bring him the head of Medusa the Gorgon.

The Gorgons were fearsome monsters who lived on an unknown island in the north. All were immortal except the youngest, Medusa. They were so horrible-looking that any mortal who saw them would be turned to stone.

Perseus started off on his quest, but had no idea where to go. Fortunately, Hermes and Athena decided to help him and gave him three gifts. Hermes gave Perseus a sword that could cut through the Gorgon's scales and a bag that would fit whatever was put into it. Athena loaned Perseus her shield which was so highly polished that it was like a mirror, so Perseus would not have to look at the Gorgons but could see them in the shield. Hades loaned him his helmet which would make the wearer invisible, and Hermes donated his wings. But how to get to the Gorgons, they did not tell him. To find out where they lived, he had to visit the Gray Ones.

The Gray Ones were three ugly women who had only one eye among them. As they passed it from one to the other, Perseus snatched it out of their hands and refused to give it back until they told him where the Gorgons lived. They quickly gave him the information and he returned the eye.

At last he arrived at the home of the Gorgons.

When they were asleep, he put on all the gifts of the gods and, looking into the shield, cut off the head of Medusa. He quickly dropped the head into his bag and flew south.

But on the way, another adventure awaited him. Cassiopeia, the queen of Ethiopia, had been foolish enough to claim that she was more beautiful than the Nereides, the sea nymphs. Poseidon sent a sea monster to kill the people of her country in punishment for this claim. An oracle told the Ethiopians that the only way they could be saved would be to sacrifice the queen's daughter Andromeda to the sea monster.

So the queen and the king took Andromeda to the seashore and bound her to a rock to wait for the sea monster. But as she was waiting there, Perseus passed by on his way home. Dropping to earth with his winged sandals and taking off the helmet so he could be seen, he asked who she was and what was the problem.

She didn't have to answer because just then the huge sea monster lunged out of the water after his prey. Perseus swooped down on him and stabbed him with his sword. Then he rescued the lovely Andromeda, and asked her parents for her hand in marriage. They could not refuse, so she went back with him to Polydectes.

When he returned home he found that his mother and the fisherman Dictys were in danger from Polydectes who was still trying to marry Danaë. So Perseus went to the palace where Polydectes was holding a banquet. As he walked into the hall, everyone looked up in amazement that he had returned. And while they were all looking at him, he reached into his bag and held aloft the head of Medusa, and all were turned to stone.

His countrymen were delighted to be freed from the tyrant Polydectes, and Dictys the kind fisherman became their new king. Perseus returned his gifts to the gods and gave Athena Medusa's head to wear on her shield.

Gorgon (from Gorgon, a monster of Greek mythology so ugly that anyone who looked at it would turn to stone): a repulsive or ugly woman

hercules

GREEK

Herculean (from Hercules, Greek hero): of great size or strength

Hercules was the son of Zeus, and thus was the enemy of Hera. When he was still an infant, Hera sent two huge serpents crawling into his crib to kill him. But the next morning when his nurse looked in on him she found the infant Hercules playing with the bodies of the two snakes which he had strangled.

While he was still young, Hercules married the beautiful princess Megara and they had three sons. But Hera chose this time to inflict upon him the worst punishment she had ever devised. She made him go mad, and while crazy he killed his wife and three sons. When he came to his senses, he was horrified to find their bodies surrounding him and to see the blood of his own sons.

"How can I live?" Hercules cried in despair and rushed out to kill himself. But suddenly Theseus hurried up to him and stopped him.

"You were mad, Hercules. It was a deed of the gods. Be strong in your suffering, for that is the fate of mankind," Theseus said.

Overcome by his friend's kindness, Hercules did decide against suicide, but he went to the oracle of Apollo to try to find some way of being cleansed of his crime. The oracle told him to go to his cousin Eurystheus, the king of Mycenae, and submit to whatever deeds he required of him.

Obviously Eurystheus was an ideal person for the task, for few humans could have thought up such an array of difficult jobs, though of course he may have had the aid of Hera in devising some of the most diabolical tasks. In all, he came up with twelve tasks which Her-

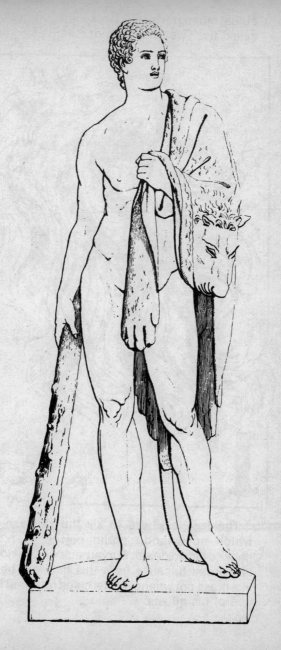

159

cules must perform. These are sometimes called the Twelve Labors of Hercules.

1

The first task was to kill the Nemean lion which no weapon could pierce. Hercules choked him to death. Eurystheus was obviously impressed because from this time on, he hid in a brass pot whenever Hercules returned from one of his quests.

The second task was to kill a creature with nine heads called the Hydra. What made the Hydra such a challenge was that whenever one head was cut off, two would grow in its place. Hercules took a friend this time, who quickly burned the stump whenever Hercules cut a head off so the new heads could not grow back.

The third task was to bring back alive a stag with golden horns which was sacred to Artemis. It took Hercules a whole year to catch it, and then Artemis snatched it away from him. But after he pleaded with her, she allowed him to take it.

The Erymanthian boar was a very fierce animal which Hercules also had to bring back alive. This time he hunted the animal in the winter and finally trapped it in very deep snow.

The fifth labor was to clean the stables of King Augeus, who had hundreds of cattle and oxen and never cleaned up after them. Rather than get into all that mess, Hercules diverted two rivers whose waters carried away all of the filth.

The sixth labor was to chase off the Stymphalian birds which plagued the people of Stymphalus. Athena helped him to shoot these birds.

The seventh labor was to bring the bull that Poseidon had given King Minos, a bull that according to other legends was the father of the Minotaur.

The eighth labor was to capture the man-eating mares of King Diomedes of Thrace. Hercules supposedly fed their master to them and then had no trouble mastering them. But on his way to fulfill this task, Hercules happened onto one of his other adventures. On his way he stopped at the home of King Admetus, whose wife had just died.

The cause of her death was rather strange. An oracle had prophesied that Admetus himself would die unless someone could be found who would exchange his life for that of the king. But no one would agree to this—not even the king's old father. Finally Alcestis, the queen, offered her life.

Hercules arrived in the middle of the funeral rites, but was so insensitive that he did not realize anything was wrong. Admetus entertained him very hospitably and tried to keep the bad news from him. Hercules dined alone

167

in his room and became drunk and sang all kinds of obscene songs. Finally one of the servants told him of the death of the queen.

Hercules was horrified and wondered what he could do to make up for his horrible behavior. There was only one deed that could right it. He must bring Alcestis back from the dead.

So Hercules rushed off to the tomb and found death just leaving. Even Death himself could not withstand Hercules' powerful grasp and finally agreed to return Alcestis. Then the whole house rejoiced and got drunk to celebrate.

But Hercules had to return to his labors. The ninth labor was to obtain the girdle of Queen

Hippolyta of the Amazons. According to most stories, he had to kill her to get the girdle, but some storytellers remembered that Hippolyta married Hercules' friend Theseus and decided that Hercules must have kidnapped her and given her to Theseus after taking her girdle.

The tenth labor was to bring the cattle of Geryon, a monster who lived on Erythia, an island far to the west. To commemorate this labor, Hercules set up the Pillars of Hercules—now called the Rock of Gibraltar—to mark the end of the sea.

Obtaining the golden apples of the Hesperides was the eleventh thing Hercules had to do. No one knew where to find them, but since Atlas was the father of the Hesperides, Hercules thought he might help. On his way to find Atlas, Hercules happened to see Prometheus still chained to the mountain with a vulture pecking at his liver. Hercules didn't care if Zeus himself had imposed the punishment. He smote the chains that bound the great Titan and set him free.

Then he went on to Atlas, another unfortunate Titan whom Zeus had punished by making him hold up the heavens. Hercules found him in the middle of Africa and asked if he could tell him where the apples of the Hesperides were.

Atlas (from Atlas, Greek god forced to bear the world on his shoulders): 1. a person who bears a heavy burden 2. a collection of maps of the world

---

"I cannot tell you," replied Atlas craftily. "I would be glad to try to get them for you, but if I move, the heavens will fall in. However, if you would hold it for me, I would go."

Hercules, who was not too bright, agreed.

Surprisingly, Atlas returned with the apples, but said that now he would go off and take them to Eurystheus and leave Hercules holding the heavens.

"Very well. You win," Hercules said. "But if I am going to have to stay here forever, please hold up the heavens for just a minute while I put a pad on my shoulders.

Atlas agreed and, of course, as soon as he took the burden from Hercules' back, Hercules picked up the apples and ran off.

But Hercules was not finished. The twelfth labor was to go to Hades itself and bring back Cerberus, the three-headed dog that guards the underworld. Hades must have admired his great strength, for he let Hercules bring back not only Cerberus but his cousin Theseus, who had attempted to kidnap Persephone, as well.

The twelve labors were over, but Hercules' troubles were not. Hercules now fell in love with a princess named Deianeira. To win her, he had to fight the river god Achelous who changed himself into a bull. Hercules tore off

12

the bull's horn, and the river nymphs took it from him and filled it with fruits. It became the cornucopia, or horn of plenty.

Hercules' life with Deianeira was pleasant for a while. But one day as they were crossing a river where there was no bridge, a centaur offered to carry Deianeira across on his back so she would not get wet. As soon as they were across, the centaur galloped off with Hercules' wife. Hercules shot him with a poisoned arrow.

As the centaur was dying, he pretended to

be sorry for his crime and offered to atone for it by giving Deianeira a charm.

"Take a vial of my blood," he said, "and if Hercules ever begins to stray away from you, this charm will make all of his love return to you." Deianeira did as she was told, for she knew that Hercules' eyes sometimes strayed from her.

Sure enough, sometime later, one of Hercules' old girl friends, Iole, appeared, and Deianeira remembered the charm. She sprinkled the blood on one of Hercules' robes.

But when he put it on, instead of making him fall in love with her, it scorched and scarred his body with a terrible poison. It was as if he were continually engulfed in flames. But he could not die. He begged his friend Philoctetes to build a funeral pyre and burn his body.

Zeus finally remembered his son and decided that he had suffered enough. He brought him to heaven and made him immortal. Hera, herself, agreed that his punishment had been sufficient and even gave him her daughter Hebe as a wife.

The forbidden fruit—the fruit of guilt through experience, knowledge through experience—had to be swallowed in the Garden of Innocence before human history could begin. Evil had to be accepted and assimilated, not avoided.

HEINRICH ZIMMER

The most popular myths usually deal with strong men fighting strange demons, but in these myths there is the suggestion that the real struggle is within every man himself—a struggle between different elements in his nature. Dionysus, the god of the wine that releases man's inhibitions and allows both his evil and good nature to be expressed, is an excellent example of this inner struggle.

dionysus

A flash of lightning, a cry of pain, and a god was born. Zeus, the king of the gods, came to a mortal woman, Semele, and made her pregnant. A proud woman, Semele begged to see her lover in his supernatural form and refused to listen to Zeus' claims that no mortal could look on him and live. She continued to plead, and at last Zeus, losing his patience, appeared before her in all of his glory. Poor Semele saw only a flash of lightning before she was burned to a crisp by the heat, but Zeus took the unborn child from her womb and sewed it into his thigh where he kept it for nine months until it was ready to be born.

Dionysus was born from Zeus' thigh complete with horns and a crown of serpents and was so conceited that he immediately climbed up onto his father's throne and started playing with Zeus' lightning. Zeus looked at his young son in amusement, but Hera came running in, angrily demanding to know who this new illegitimate child of her husband was.

"So Semele is dead," she replied, after hearing the story. "At least you won't be seeing her any more. But I surely hope you don't plan to let this horned monstrosity play around your throne like an important god.''

Zeus was used to Hera's biting tongue and ignored her, but this time Hera did more than talk. She went to the Titans and asked their help in doing away with this silly-looking upstart. A few days later, while Dionysus was looking at himself in a mirror, the Titans crept up on him to kill him.

Dionysian (from Dionysus, Greek god of wine): orgiastic, sensuous, or frenzied

---

Suddenly the infant Dionysus caught a glimpse of one of the Titans in the mirror. Instantly he was no longer a toddling child but a fierce lion facing his enemies. The Titans started back at seeing the god in this strange form, but they soon recovered and closed in again. Desperate, Dionysus then turned himself into a horse, then a serpent, and last a bull, but could not escape from the persistent Titans. Finally their spears hit him, and while still in the form of a bull, he died.

Hera, however, was not satisfied. She had seen gods rise from the dead before. So she had the Titans tear the body limb from limb and boil it in a cauldron. But all of Hera's precautions were in vain. Zeus took the mutilated remains of his delightful little son to his venerable mother, Rhea, and she put him back together and gave him life again.

Zeus now knew better than to take Dionysus back to Olympus, so he took him to his mother's sister, Queen Ino, who agreed to raise him as a girl in the women's quarters. But Hera was not easily fooled. She found him there and drove Ino and her husband mad. Zeus rescued Dionysus just in time, and this time changed him into a goat and sent him to live with the nymphs on Mount Nysa. While he was there, Dionysus, who is also called Bacchus, invented wine.

Dionysus not only invented wine, he used it. He drank and drank until he went into fits of ecstasy. And when Hera found him again she used his own discovery to punish him, for she made him drink so much that he went mad.

Alternating between madness and ecstasy, Dionysus wandered around the world spreading his cult of wine and wild orgies. He had a magical attraction for women, and soon he was followed by a band of wild females who left their husbands and children for a life of ecstasy and savagery. Soon satyrs—half-goat, half-human creatures—also joined his wild throng. He traveled throughout the world from India to Greece to Egypt, spreading his gift of wine and followed by frenzied women who came to be called maenads.

Bacchanal (from Bacchus, Latin name for the Greek god of wine): a drunken feast or orgy

---

Those who opposed his worship—and there were many, for he upset order and civilized life—suffered a horrible fate. Lycurgus was the first powerful king to oppose him. With his army, he surrounded Dionysus and his maenads and captured all of the women. But Dionysus drove him mad and he killed his own son with an ax. Dionysus warned the horror-stricken people that their land would be barren until Lycurgus was killed, so they took their king to Mount Parnassus where they tied him to wild horses who pulled his body apart.

Next Dionysus came to the country of his cousin, King Pentheus, where he again began spreading his rites. At first Pentheus treated him well, but when all of the women from his court began to roam the countryside, dancing and taking part in wild, obscene orgies, he became angry and decided to arrest Dionysus. This time Dionysus drove the women mad and made them think that Pentheus was a wild animal. Led by Pentheus' mother, Agave, they tore him limb from limb.

No one is certain exactly what all of the rites of Dionysus consisted of, but apparently the death of King Pentheus was not an unusual occurrence. There are suggestions that tearing animals apart limb from limb in memory of the way Dionysus was dismembered by Hera was a frequent part of the rituals, and that human beings may occasionally have been the victims.

But there was more to the worship of Dionysus than savagery. There was also the ecstasy and a sense of communication with higher powers. It was Dionysus who gave Greeks a hope for immortality, perhaps because of his own death and resurrection. Some of the Greeks celebrated the return of Dionysus and his mother from Hades in an annual festival. Eventually the great Dionysia of Athens was the scene of the beginning of Greek drama.

After his worship was established in Greece, Dionysus went to the island of Naxos. There he found a beautiful girl weeping uncontrollably. It was Ariadne, who had fled from her home in Crete with Theseus and had then been ignominiously left behind. Dionysus fell in love with her, and Ariadne quickly forgot Theseus for the love of this strange but powerful and handsome god. For a marriage present, Dionysus gave his bride a golden crown and held a great celebration. But the god, with all of his powers, could not make his wife immortal, and at last

Ariadne died. The grief-stricken god took the golden crown from her head and flung it into the heavens where it turned into stars and remains to this day.

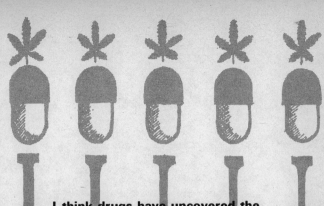

I think drugs have uncovered the unconscious depths in a society that is lopsidedly rational and evaluative. . . . But there has been too much violence and frenzy in all of this. The young seem bewildered by the world of the psyche. They came into it too fast. It is like the situation in Greek mythology in which a person says to a god, "Show me yourself in your full power" and the god does and the person is blown to bits.

JOSEPH CAMPBELL

THE INNER QUEST

The outer quest of the hero is symbolic of the inner quest of every man to find and overthrow or reconcile the evil monsters within himself and to release the spiritual energy which will enable him to lead a successful life. A young Sioux fasted and tortured himself in a lonely quest for a vision that would give him a power to become a warrior. A Yaqui sorcerer spent years learning to use and control the strange powers released by dangerous drugs. A Tibetan yogi spent years of discipline learning to control his outer senses so that he could reach the powers of the dimension beyond the worlds of the senses.

In our own culture, Sigmund Freud developed psychoanalysis to help his patients reach beyond their rational world into the subconscious, where he felt tremendous energy was stored. Freud believed that by understanding the drives and desires hidden in his subconscious, a person would be able to function more successfully.

Freud and many of his successors believe that both dreams and myths are ways for a person's subconscious mind to speak to him. Dreams and myths express the things that people are normally afraid to talk about, by conveying their message in a story and in symbols, instead of telling it directly. To most of us, death, evil, sex, and incest are frightening even to think about—and almost impossible to talk about. It is not surprising, therefore, that these are among the most common topics in myths and dreams. Myths and dreams help us to understand and deal with the things that we are too frightened to think about rationally.

For example, Freud thought that most boys go through a stage of being sexually attracted to their mothers and wanting to kill their fathers. This, of course, is a very frightening idea and contradicts everything that the child wants to believe about himself. Freud found this idea fairly common in myths and named these feelings after the most famous myth about them, the story of Oedipus, a man who killed his father and married his mother.

If Freud is right and myths are the expression of unconscious feelings that people have, then the study of mythology can be very useful in helping us to understand ourselves better. The study of mythology, like the Sioux's fast or the shaman's drugs, can help us to discover our own hidden internal monsters and can give us the power to overcome them.

Primitive myths and rituals allow their followers to understand, express, and overcome these impulses which society cannot allow to be acted upon. Among the Iatmul of New Guinea, as on every other continent, male initiation rites and myths teach young boys the roles expected of them as adult men, and allow ceremonial expression of the unconscious feelings the boy has toward his mother and father. Through frightening, painful ceremonies, which include circumcision and scarification, the fathers communicate

181

to their sons the masculine power which Freud thought the young man wanted to symbolically kill his father to obtain.

The myths of the initiation rites show that these secret powers originally belonged to the women. So by learning the secret myths and passing through the rites, the young boys satisfy their unconscious need to obtain the power of their fathers and to transfer their desire for their mothers to a desire for appropriate wives.

We, who have to a great extent lost faith in the myths of our culture and relegated our sacred rites to commercial holidays, must find new ways of releasing the powers within our own subconscious. Through psychoanalysis, through our dreams, or through our own cultural mediums of music, dance, drama, and movies, we seek to discover our quest, tame our monsters, and integrate our personalities.

In a pluralistic culture . . . every individual must create a private mythological system. I must discover within myself the Garden of Eden from which I am exiled and the New Jerusalem toward which I am journeying. And must bear the burden of being my own redeemer, my own Christ.

SAM KEEN

HOW HIGH CAN MAN FLY?

Man does not always win his quests. Sometimes the hero loses because he is too weak and the task must wait for a stronger man. But sometimes the task itself may be too great. Throughout history man has been very sensitive to his limits and to the differences between himself and his god. Only in the past fifty years has man begun to feel that his only limit is himself.

And they said, Go to, let us build us a city and a tower, whose top may reach unto heaven; and let us make us a name, lest we be scattered abroad upon the face of the whole earth.

And the Lord came down to see the city and the tower, which the children of men builded.

And the Lord said, Behold, the people is one, and they have all one language; and this they begin to do; and now nothing will be restrained from them, which they have imagined to do.

Go to, let us go down, and there confound their language, that they may not understand one another's speech.

So the Lord scattered them abroad from thence upon the face of all the earth; and they left off to build the city.

GENESIS 11:4-8

trisanku

There was once a king named Trisanku who decided that he wanted to ascend to heaven in his bodily form. So he went to his family priest and asked for help in achieving this feat.

"I have never heard anything so ridiculous in my life," replied the priest.

"You are my priest and you are supposed to do what I want you to!" yelled Trisanku angrily. "If you don't do the proper sacrifices and ceremonies to make me ascend into heaven, you and your family will be in serious trouble!"

The priest, of course, still refused. "You are not even worthy of being a king, let alone going to heaven," said the priest. "I pray to the gods that you will lose your kingly caste and be made a member of the lowest caste, a chandala!"

Trisanku was horrified by this disaster and immediately embarked on a pilgrimage to find a priest who could restore his caste to him. He soon met the great yogi, Viswamitra, who was at that very moment looking for some task that would enable him to demonstrate his powers.

"I'll not only restore your caste," Viswamitra boasted, "I'll get you into heaven, too."

So Viswamitra made a great sacrifice and began a period of ten days of meditation and fasting. At the end of ten days, Trisanku began very slowly to rise above the earth. He gradually began to gain speed and soon shot out of sight. People had gathered from all of India to see this great sight, and they stood looking up in amazement at the powers of Viswamitra.

But suddenly a speck appeared above them in the sky and soon they could make out the figure of Trisanku descending just as rapidly as he had risen. Viswamitra immediately began to meditate again and the great powers of his mind managed to stop Trisanku just before he reached the ground. But Trisanku was upside-down.

"What happened?" cried Viswamitra.

"I got all the way up to heaven," moaned Trisanku, "but Indra kicked me right back out headfirst because he said I was a chandala."

Viswamitra was angry. "I am not going to lose this challenge," he muttered and immediately began building sacrificial fires and concentrating his powerful mind.

"Please," pleaded poor Trisanku. "I don't want to go to heaven again. I don't even want to be a king. Just put me on my feet again, and I will be content." But even as he was speaking, he began to rise through the power of Viswamitra's fierce concentration.

No sooner had he risen out of sight than he fell back down again. This time Viswamitra was furious.

"I'll show Indra!" he said. "If he won't let you into his heaven, I'll create your own heaven for you!"

"Just let me down," cried poor Trisanku.

"Nonsense," said Viswamitra, and he began the most tremendous concentration ever. Soon Trisanku, still upside-down, began to rise again, but this time in a slightly different direction. The amazed people watching saw a new star appear in the heavens. "It is Trisanku's heaven!" they cried.

But the last words poor Trisanku was heard to say were, "Please turn me right-side-up!"

"Don't worry," called Viswamitra, "I've created your heaven upside-down!"

PERHAPS THE GODS WERE SPACE MEN

Erich Von Daniken in *Chariots of the Gods* poses the interesting suggestion that most of the world's myths are primitive accounts of actual events in the distant past when the earth was visited by astronauts from a distant planet.

Indeed, almost all mythologies teem with accounts of gods flying to earth from their distant home in the heavens and of heroes who fly with the gods to the sun or the moon or the stars. A myth of the Carib Indians even claims that they are descendants of people who originally inhabited the moon and were sent to clean up the earth. A legend from Tiahuanaco in South America states that the Earth Mother came down from the heavens to give birth to mankind. And Tiahuanaco, located in the remote mountains of Bolivia, has tangible evidence for its claims of a supernatural origin! Gigantic ruins of sixty-ton stone blocks and six-foot-long pieces of stone forming a carefully crafted water conduit make it almost as easy to believe these to be the works of supernaturals or beings from outer space as the work of primitive men.

Similar myths and art styles in distant, apparently unrelated cultures have long puzzled scholars. Some have suggested that these similarities, particularly the striking likeness between the art and architecture of the Middle East, the South Sea Islands, and South America, were the result of migration. Von Daniken suggests that all three cultures were started by space visitors who taught them their skills, myths, and art.

The fascination of primitive people with astronomy, the fantastic astronomical calculations of the Mayans and Aztecs, and the almost universal concept of astrology could all support Daniken's hypothesis.

An interesting fantasy? Who knows? Maybe earth man will someday be god in the myths of some primitive species on some still distant and unknown planet.

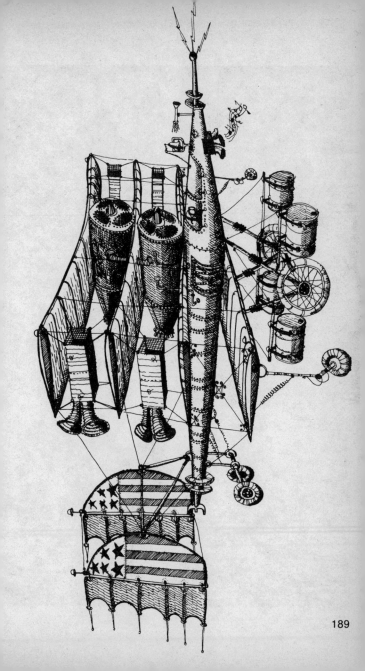

189

OR MAYBE WE'LL FLY TOO HIGH

Daedalus, who created the Labyrinth for King Minos, and then helped Theseus escape from it, was punished by the king for his role in Theseus' exploits. King Minos imprisoned the clever architect and his son Icarus in his own Labyrinth, and Daedalus did not have time to get a ball of string to help him find his way out.

But Daedalus was too clever for King Minos, for he knew he could still escape through the air. He made wings for himself and his son out of wax and bird feathers. Before they left, he warned his son not to fly too high or the sun would melt the wax and the wings would fall off.

But Icarus was young and headstrong and disregarded his father's advice. As they were flying over the sea, he flew too high, the wings melted, and he fell into the sea.

The distraught father succeeded in his flight and went to Sicily, but apparently never again attempted to fly.

THE EXISTENTIAL HERO

The standard hero in mythology is the killer of the monster, like Theseus or Perseus, the doer of impossible deeds, like Hercules, the dreamer of impossible dreams, like Trisanku, and the perfect personification of morals and cultural values, like Arjuna.

But there is another mythological pattern for the hero, popular among American Indians, Africans, and Asians, and more evident than we frequently admit in European mythology. This is the trickster-hero or scamp, the existential hero who comes to terms with the monster within him, who compromises the values of his culture with the practical problems of life, and who has no aspirations beyond enjoying his life on this earth.

Albert Camus pictures this kind of hero in *The Myth of Sisyphus* as a man who knows that his fate is inevitably death, that the great deeds that he does will come to nothing, that he has little control over his own destiny, but who resolves to take control over himself and, defying the universe, lives in joy. Sisyphus, a man who refused to obey the immortals, was condemned in Hades to push a rock up a hill for eternity. As soon as the rock reached the top of the hill, it rolled back down and Sisyphus was forced to begin again.

Thus is the life of the trickster-hero, the man with his eyes open. He knows that killing the dragon has no ultimate meaning, but he kills him anyway and even invents more enemies to fight with. He knows that cultural mores have little meaning and either openly flaunts customs or good-humoredly goes along with them.

He is a man, a human being, a highly evolved animal whose habitation is the earth, and he is determined to make the best of it.

He who assists the ruler with Tao does not dominate the world with force.
The use of force usually brings requital.
Wherever armies are stationed, briers and thorns grow.
Great wars are always followed by famines.
A good general achieves his purpose and stops, but dares not seek to dominate the world.
He achieves his purpose but does not brag about it.
He achieves his purpose but does not boast about it.
He achieves his purpose but is not proud of it.
He achieves his purpose but only as an unavoidable step.
He achieves his purpose but does not aim to dominate.

THE WAY OF LAO TSU, TRANSLATED BY WING-TSIT CHAN (BOBBS MERRILL CO., 1963)

My faith in human dignity consists in the belief that man is the greatest scamp on earth. Human dignity must be associated with the idea of a scamp and not with that of an obedient, disciplined, and regimented soldier. The scamp is probably the most glorious type of human being, as the soldier is the lowest type, according to this conception.

LIN YUTANG

It makes one's heart ache when one sees that a man has staked his soul upon some end, the hopeless imperfection and futility of which is immediately obvious to everyone but himself. But isn't this, after all, merely a matter of degree? Isn't the pathetic grandeur of human existence in some way bound up with the eternal disproportion in this world, where self-delusion is necessary to life, between the honesty and the striving and the nullity of the result? That we all—every one of us—take ourselves seriously is not merely ridiculous.

DAG HAMMARSKJÖLD

Speaking as a Chinese, I do not think that any civilization can be called complete until it has progressed from sophistication to unsophistication, and made a conscious return to simplicity of thinking and living, and I call no man wise until he has made the progress from the wisdom of knowledge to the wisdom of foolishness, and become a laughing philosopher, feeling first life's tragedy and then life's comedy. For we must weep before we can laugh. Out of sadness comes the awakening and out of the awakening comes the laughter of the philosopher, with kindliness and tolerance to boot.

LIN YUTANG

truth and falsehood

Fene-Falsehood and Deug-Truth started out on a journey one day.

Fene-Falsehood said, "Everyone says that the Lord loves truth better than falsehood, so I think that you had better do all the talking for us."

Deug-Truth agreed, and when they came to a village, Deug-Truth greeted the first woman they met and asked if they could have a drink. She gave them a filthy bowl full of lukewarm water and then sat down in the doorway of her hut and began to eat a big meal of rice. While the two travelers were still there, the woman's husband came home and asked for his supper.

"It's not ready," replied the woman insolently.

The husband then turned to the two strangers who were watching and asked, "What would you say about a woman like that?"

"I would say that she is the worst wife I have seen in a long time. It's bad enough for her not to be hospitable to strangers, but it is really disgraceful when she doesn't feed her own husband," replied Deug-Truth. Fene-Falsehood didn't say a word.

The woman became furious and began to yell and scream louder than either of the two travelers had ever heard anyone scream before. "Are you going to stand by and let these strangers insult me!" she screamed to her husband. "If so, I will go home to my father and you will have to raise a bride-price for a new wife."

Then the husband, too, became angry and

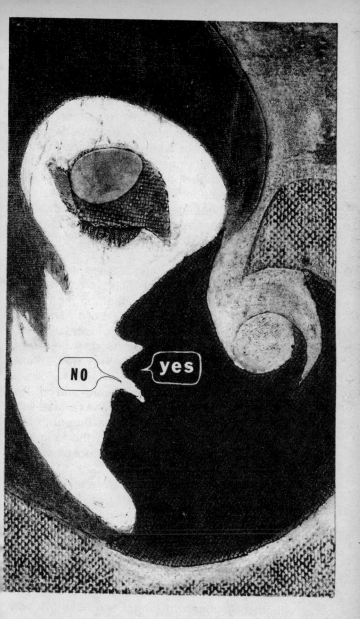

chased the two strangers out of town.

So Deug and Fene continued their travels and next came to a village where they found several children dividing up a bull that had just been slaughtered. They thought that this was rather strange, for it was the custom that meat was always divided by the head-man. While they were still watching, they saw the chief come up and take a very poor share of meat which the children handed him. The chief saw the two strangers and asked, "Who do you think is the leader in this village?"

Fene said nothing but Deug immediately answered, "It seems to me that these children must be the leaders of this village, for they are dividing the meat."

The chief immediately became angry and chased them out of that village.

As they continued to walk along, Fene said to Deug, "It is said that the Lord loves you the best, but I am beginning to wonder if man is not rather different from God. It seems to me that men do not like you very well. I think I will try my luck at the next village."

At the next village, they found that all the people were weeping because the favorite wife of the king had just died. Fene thought for a minute and then said, "Go tell the king that a man is here who can raise people from the dead."

Soon Fene was brought before the king and said, "I will raise your wife from the dead if you will give me half of your fortune."

The king immediately agreed and Fene had a hut built above the family grave. The king and all of the people waited outside and listened to the strange noises. First they heard huffing and panting and strange chants, but then they began to hear Fene talking loudly as if he were arguing. Finally he burst out of the door and slammed it shut—holding it tightly.

"Oh, dear," he said, "you did not tell me that your whole family was buried in there. When I woke your wife up, your father and your grandfather both came out too. I thought I had better check before I let them all out."

The king and his advisers began to look frightened, for the king's father had been a very cruel king and the new king and his friends had given his death a little assistance.

"I think you had better leave them all," said the king. "We would have a lot of trouble here with three kings."

"Well, it's not that easy," said Fene slyly. "Your father has offered me half of his property to let him out. I am certainly not going to send him back for nothing."

"I will still give you half of my property," said the desperate king. "Just get rid of them all."

So Fene received half of the king's fortune and concluded that while truth might have the favor of God, falsehood was the best way to get ahead with men.

halid the scamp

There was once a young man named Halid who lived by his wits. One day he took a friend named Osman and went to a nearby city. As soon as they arrived in the marketplace, Halid feigned a terrible heart attack and fell down, pretending to be dead. Osman covered his face with a sack and sat beside him to mourn the sad fate of the stranger who had died in this city and had no money for burial.

The passersby were touched by this sad story and contributed generously to the burial fund. Just as Halid was about to decide that they had gotten enough money, the grand vizier himself came by. When he heard the story, he told an imam standing by to take the corpse

200

and bury it and then to come and collect the expenses.

So Halid was carried off to the mosque, and Osman went home with the money. The imam laid Halid out on the floor and went off to get the necessary materials. But as soon as he was gone, Halid jumped up and put on the imam's cloak and turban and ran out. He immediately went to the vizier to ask for the payment for burying the stranger.

Of course, it was only a few minutes later when the real imam came to tell about the corpse that had disappeared. The vizier immediately set the best detective on Halid's trail.

The next day the detective saw Halid and began to chase him. Halid darted into an apothecary shop and said, "My uncle, who will soon come in looking for me, is crazy. If you will pour water all over his head and hold him down for half an hour, he will regain his sanity. Here is money to pay for the treatment."

Of course, the detective came in a few minutes later asking for Halid, and was immediately subjected to the water treatment. Since he persisted in his delusions that he was not Halid's uncle but a detective, the apothecary held him down longer than the required half hour.

After several weeks of similar escapades, Halid was captured in the middle of the night by a group of soldiers. The soldiers decided to tie him to a tree rather than stay awake and guard him until morning. But Halid stayed awake, and soon he saw an old hunchback man coming toward him.

"Sir," he whispered loudly. "Come here quickly and tell me if it is gone."

"What?" asked the old man.

"See if my hump is gone," replied Halid.

"There certainly is no hump on your back," replied the old hunchback.

"Then the treatment worked, praise Allah!" said Halid. "Please untie me, then."

"Well," said the old man, thinking he was being very clever. "I will untie you if you will tell me what the secret that got rid of your hump is."

"It is very simple," said Halid. "You must be tied to this tree and repeat three secret words a hundred times. The words are 'Esserti! Pesserti! Sersepeti!' "

The hunchback quickly untied Halid and Halid then tied him to the tree. The next morning, instead of Halid, the soldiers found only an old hunchback who would say nothing except three nonsense words.

When the vizier heard this tale. he was so amused that he decided to pardon Halid and sent a messenger through the streets proclaiming pardon for Halid if he would come to the palace. And when Halid arrived, the vizier made him his chief detective.

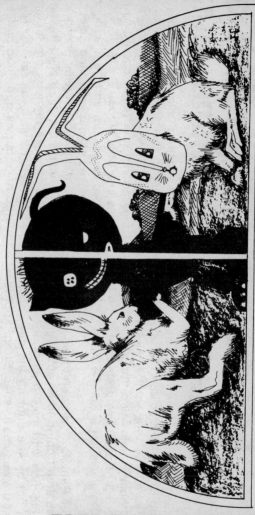

br'er rabbit and tar baby

One summer when everything was dry, Br'er Fox and Br'er Bear decided that they needed to dig a well. So they went to all the animals to ask them to help. All of the animals agreed except Br'er Rabbit. He pretended to be sick, but the animals knew that he wasn't. So they said,

"Br'er Rabbit, if you don't help us dig this well, we aren't going to let you drink from it."

"That's fine with me," replied Br'er Rabbit. "I can get by fine drinking the dew." But as soon as the well was finished, Br'er Rabbit went out every night and drank from it.

The other animals became very angry and decided to try to catch Br'er Rabbit and punish him. Finally they decided to make an animal out of wood and cover it with tar.

rabbit and birdlime animal

The rabbit and the antelope were once building a well. Early in the morning they both set out with their lunches for the work site. As soon as they arrived, the rabbit offered to put the lunches in a cool place.

The two began to work, but suddenly the rabbit pricked up his ears and said, "I hear people from the village calling me."

"I don't hear a thing," replied the antelope.

"That's because my ears are longer and I can hear better," said the rabbit. "My wife is about to have babies and I had better go."

And the rabbit scampered off to the spot where he had hidden the lunches and ate part of them.

The same thing happened three times during the day, and the rabbit explained that his wife had had several children.

That afternoon when the antelope was ready to eat his lunch, the rabbit went to get it and cried, "Oh, a cat has been here before us and has already eaten our food."

The second day the rabbit played the same trick on the antelope, and this continued until the well was almost finished. Finally the antelope realized what was happening and followed the rabbit. He caught him red-handed with the lunches.

"You have tricked me," yelled the antelope. "I should kill you, but I won't. But to pay for the lunches, you must give me full rights to the well and promise never to drink from it."

The frightened rabbit agreed. But the well had hardly been completed when the antelope began noticing rabbit tracks around it. "That pesky rabbit is trying to trick me again," thought the antelope. "I will show him who is the cleverest."

So the antelope took a piece of wood and

They set the tar baby up by the well, and when Br'er Rabbit came for his drink, he saw that someone was guarding the well.

"Who's there?" he called from the bushes. But the tar baby didn't answer.

"I said, who's there?" said the rabbit, getting bolder and coming out of the bushes. The rabbit walked right up to the tar baby and said in its face, "If you don't answer me, I am going to hit you." But the tar baby didn't say a word.

So the rabbit hit him with his right hand and it stuck. Then he hit him with his left hand and it stuck. Then he hit him with his feet and they both stuck. Soon the rabbit was completely stuck and the other animals came out and picked him up.

"Let's roast him alive," said the fox.

"That's fine with me," said Br'er Rabbit. "I like to be nice and warm and my coat won't burn at all."

"That doesn't sound very good," said Br'er Bear. "Let's hang him from a tree."

205

"That would be fun," said Br'er Rabbit. "I am so light I could just swing there and enjoy myself."

"That's no good," said Br'er Possum. "Let's throw him in the bramble bush."

Then Br'er Rabbit started to scream. "Don't throw me in there. I am scared of the brambles. They will stick my feet and my eyes!"

While he was still screaming, all the animals picked him up and threw him in the briar patch. As soon as he was safe in the brambles, Br'er Rabbit yelled back, "Thanks a lot. You have thrown me right back to my home!"

carved it into an animal about the size of the rabbit. Then he stuck the wooden animal in the ground near the well and smeared it all over with birdlime.

Soon the rabbit came hopping up. He saw the figure standing there and said, "What are you doing at my well?"

The wooden figure of course said nothing. The rabbit became angry and said, "Answer me or I will hit you."

The wooden figure was still silent and the rabbit hit it with his right hand. His hand stuck.

"Let me go or I will hit you again," the rabbit shouted. Nothing happened and he hit the figure with both back legs and they stuck. Then he butted it with his head and his stomach. Soon the silly rabbit was completely stuck.

Just then the antelope came up. "So there you are, you silly rabbit," he said. "You will never trick anyone again." And he killed him on the spot.

One of the greatest heroes of all mythology is Odysseus, a man who was both a scamp and a dragon-slayer.

odysseus

GREEK

Odyssey (from Odysseus, Greek hero who wandered for ten years): a long, wandering journey

For ten years the Trojan War had raged, and now it had been over for ten years more, but Penelope still waited in Ithaca for Odysseus to return. Telemachus, her son, had been only a baby when his father left, and now he was a man. Penelope for twenty years had fended off a hundred suitors who came every day to eat at her house and to continue feasting until she married one of them.

Odysseus was just as lonely after these years, if not as faithful, for he was a prisoner of a goddess named Calypso, who wanted to marry him and make him immortal. But Odysseus preferred to remain a human and would rather have his own wife and home than an eternity with Calypso.

At last Athena, Odysseus' goddess, asked Zeus to send Hermes to Calypso to demand that she free Odysseus. So with Hermes' directions, Odysseus built a raft and set out for home.

But it was not to be that easy, for Poseidon, the god of the sea, hated Odysseus and, finding his enemy afloat on his ocean, Poseidon raised a storm to end all storms. Odysseus' raft shattered, so he cast off all of his clothes and began to swim. He was miles from land, and would have been lost if Ino, a kindly goddess, had not given him her sacred veil which would keep him afloat until he came to land. Even that seemed not to be enough, for he came up to a rocky island and feared he would be dashed to bits, but the goddess Athena guided him to a stream which emptied into the ocean and, with his last remaining strength, he pulled himself up on the shore.

In the meantime, Athena hurried into the town and appeared to the princess, Nausicaä, urging her to take her maidens and go down to the stream to do the wash. Early the next morning, Nausicaä remembered her dream and decided that the laundry did indeed need to be done. So she took her maidens and they went to the stream.

After the wash was finished and the clothes were spread to dry, the girls played ball in the sun. Odysseus woke up and, hearing them, decided to beg for mercy. The girls were suddenly startled to see a naked man—modestly holding a leafy branch in front of him—coming out of the forest. All of them except Nausicaä ran away. So Odysseus knelt in front of her and said, "You are so beautiful that I don't know if you are a woman or a goddess. Your father and brothers are very lucky to have such a beautiful daughter and sister, and the man who marries you will be blessed above all men. Now I pray that you will help a poor stranger and give me some clothes and tell me how to get into town."

Nausicaä was a generous girl and more than willing to help the handsome stranger. In fact, when he had dressed and washed, she began to feel quite a bit of excitement in her heart as she stared at him.

The stranger refused to go into town with the girls, for he feared that would start gossip. Instead he followed them at a little distance and came to the palace, as Nausicaä had told him to.

Calypso (from Calypso, sea nymph in Greek mythology): an improvised ballad, originating in the British West Indies

Odysseus was welcomed at the palace, for the Greeks have a strong tradition of hospitality. He was entertained by games and singing and not even asked his name. Several days later a famous minstrel came to the hall and that night he sang the songs of the tales of Troy. As he sang of the battles of Agamemnon and Achilles and of Odysseus the crafty, and the Trojan Horse, Odysseus began to weep, for he remembered his friends and companions— most of them dead—that the minstrel sang about. At last the king noticed that his guest was weeping and told the minstrel to stop.

"What is bothering you?" he asked. "Don't you like the song?"

The stranger sighed deeply and then began. "I am Odysseus. Odysseus the crafty, the inventor of the Trojan Horse. And the tales I have to tell would fill days and nights with the telling."

Encouraged by his host and by the eager Nausicaä, he told his story. "After we left Troy, we traveled many places. One of the first we saw was the land of the Lotus Eaters. In this strange place, the people eat the lotus and forget all of their troubles. Of course, before I could stop them, some of my own men ate of the lotus and they wanted to do nothing but stay in that country eating the sweet flower. Finally my other men and I had to take them as prisoners back to the boats. We left that place as quickly as we could. I was afraid that all of my men would eat the lotus and I would never get away.

"Then we came to the land of the Cyclops. They are a fierce, savage people with only one eye in their forehead. It was a strange land and I felt uneasy, so I decided to land with only one ship. From the beach we saw a huge

209

cave that seemed to be the habitation of some person, so I took twelve men and went with them, hoping that we would be welcomed and could get food and water and gifts. I took with me one of my best wineskins as a present.

"We came to the cave of this giant, but no one was home. We spied baskets of fine cheeses, and my men suggested that we simply steal some and run. But I wanted to meet the owner of the cave. I lived to regret that decision.

"That night the monster came home and he was certainly a giant. Before he even saw us, he rolled a huge stone before the door so there was no way of escape for us. Then he saw us and said, 'Well, who are you strangers? Are you pirates or adventurers?'

" 'Sir,' I said proudly, 'we are Greeks returning home from the battle of Troy. We hope you will welcome us, for you remember that Zeus protects strangers.'

"With that the huge Cyclops laughed. 'I am not afraid of Zeus. He's just a little upstart.' Having said that, he picked up two of my men and threw them against the wall so that their brains were dashed out. Then he ate them almost in a single bite. And we were forced to watch in horror.

"The next morning he let his sheep out, but before we could follow them, he replaced the heavy stone. All day we sat in the cave trying to think of a plan to escape.

"That night when he returned I offered him the wine. He drank every bit of it, and when I thought that he was drunk enough, I said, 'You haven't even asked me my name, but I'll tell it to you anyway. My name is Nobody.'

" 'Nobody, that's a funny name. Well, Nobody, since you have been so nice, I will be kind to you and eat you last.' That was his idea of generosity.

"But soon he fell asleep in a drunken stupor. When he was fast asleep, my men and I took a huge pole and sharpened it. We put it in the fire to make it hot. Then we took it to the Cyclops and drove it deep into his one huge eye. It hissed and sizzled and popped in the heat. The Cyclops screamed in agony. Then he shouted loudly for the other Cyclops.

" 'Who is hurting you?' they shouted back.

" 'Nobody is hurting me,' yelled the stupid Cyclops, not realizing why I had told him that silly name.

" 'Well, if nobody is hurting you then there is not much we can do about it,' his friends yelled back.

"The next morning the Cyclops opened the door to his cave again, but he sat right down in front of it to catch us as we tried to leave. When his sheep went out, he checked their backs to see if anyone was riding on them, but he never noticed that my men were hanging underneath them.

"As soon as we were far enough away, we jumped off and drove the sheep in front of us right down onto our ship.

"I was feeling boastful after our escape and I yelled loudly, 'Cyclops, if you ever wonder who put your eye out, you can know it was Odysseus, sacker of cities, the son of Laertes of Ithaca.'

"The Cyclops picked up a huge boulder and hurled it at the ship. The boulder missed, but he had a worse revenge for me, for he was Poseidon's son and the Earthshaker has been my enemy ever since.

"Next we landed at the island of Aeolus, god of the wind.

Aeolian (from Aeolus, Greek god of the wind): producing a soothing musical tone as though made by the wind

---

Aeolus was generous and we stayed there some time. When we left, he gave us a bag in which he had imprisoned all of the evil winds, telling me that as long as the bag was closed, we would have smooth sailing.

"But my stupid men thought that the bag held a great treasure. So while I was asleep they opened the bag and let loose all of the evil winds.

212

"Then we came to the island of the goddess Circe. Here I sent some of my men ahead to see what the land was like. They found a strange house surrounded by wolves and other ferocious beasts. The men were terrified and were glad to be invited into the house of the beautiful girl who appeared at the door. She fed them and gave them wine, but as soon as they began to drink, they began to change and turn into pigs. As soon as they were completely transformed she imprisoned them in a pigsty.

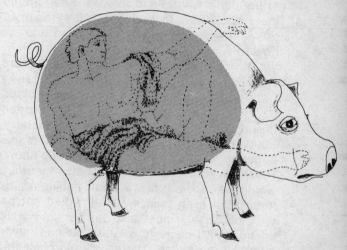

"But one man escaped, for he suspected a trap and did not go into the house with the others. He came to tell me the story. So I started off for Circe's house, but had no idea what I would do. On the way I met a young man who gave me a drug that he said would counteract her magic. It was the god Hermes who had been sent by Athena to save me. I was not forgotten by the immortals after all.

"Circe welcomed me as she had the others and gave me her wine to drink. But I took the

213

herb and drank all of her wine with no effects. Circe then raised her wand, but I drew my sword and she dropped to her knees begging for mercy.

"I granted her her life and she invited me to become her lover. But first I made her promise to work no more harm to me or my men and to free them from her spell. This she did and we stayed as her guests for a year.

"But then we became lonely for Ithaca again and set off. Before we left, Circe warned us of the perils we yet had to pass. She told me that I would have to go to the land of the dead to see the blind prophet Tiresias and told me how to succeed in the journey.

"The shores of the land of the dead were dark and dreary. I slaughtered an animal as Circe had directed me, and prepared the blood for the dead to drink. Just as she had warned me, all of the dead people began approaching, but I held them off with my sword until Tiresias appeared and told me what I wanted to know. His words bothered me. He said that my journey would be sad, but that I would finally return home. But even then my trials would not be over because I must take an oar and walk inland until I came to a land that had never heard of the ocean. There I should plant the oar and Poseidon would forgive me. He also warned us that when we came to the island of the sun we should not bother the cattle.

"Then when Tiresias finished, I talked with the other dead. My own mother was there, having died of grief when I left for Troy. It was a sad meeting. My friends from Troy, Achilles and Agamemnon, were also there with unhappy tales.

"But there were more dangers to be endured. We passed the Sirens, beautiful women whose voices lure travelers to their death on the rocks. Following Circe's advice, I stuffed my men's ears with wax, and had myself tied to the mast so I could hear their song without any danger. As we went through a narrow channel, we met Scylla and Charybdis. Scylla was a six-headed monster, and with each head she captured one of my men. We were lucky to get through with no more loss than that, for Charybdis on the other side was a giant whirlpool that could have drowned the whole ship.

"Then we came near the Island of the Sun. I did not want to stop, but we were out of water and my men insisted. I made them promise not to bother the sun god's cattle. But ill-fortune waited for us. For a whole month we were stranded there with no winds and our food gave out. At last I went inland to pray to the gods.

But while I was gone my men killed the sun god's cattle.

"No sooner had we set sail from the island than a great storm came up and destroyed my ship with all my men on it. I alone escaped. It was their punishment for killing the cattle we had been warned to leave alone.

"I was swept through the ocean for nine days before I was finally washed up on Calypso's island, and there I was a prisoner for these seven years. And now, I pray you, if my story has touched you, please send me home on a ship."

The king was touched by the story and dispatched a special ship to send Odysseus home to Ithaca. Moreover he filled the ship with precious gifts.

Odysseus was so tired and relieved to be going home that he fell asleep on the journey, and when they arrived, the sailors lifted him up still asleep and laid him gently on the shore with all of his gifts.

When he woke up, Odysseus did not know where he was, for Athena had covered the shore with a thick fog. She appeared to him disguised as a shepherd.

Odysseus was glad to see her and greeted her, asking, "What is the name of this country and what kind of people live here?"

"You must really be a stranger not to know the name of this island," said Athena. "This is fair Ithaca. Don't tell me you have never heard of it."

"Of course I have heard of it," replied Odysseus, and then, not knowing who the shepherd was, he began to lie. "Why even in my home in Crete I heard of it. I am here because I accidentally killed a man in Crete and his family was going to avenge him by killing me, so I left most of my goods with my children and fled here with only these."

Then the goddess laughed, "What a clever person it would take to trick you, Odysseus, son of Laertes." And as Odysseus stared at her, she assumed her shape as the lovely gray-eyed goddess. "But I am insulted that you did not recognize me, as much help as I have given you on your trip."

"You are cleverer than I am with disguises," Odysseus replied. "But I do certainly appreciate all that you have done for me. I know that if it were not for you, I would be at the bottom of the sea with all of my friends."

"Well, you are not safe yet," Athena said. "There are many people here in Ithaca who will not be glad to see you return. They have decided that you are lost for good and that they can divide up your land and cattle among themselves. Every day men from all over the island come to your house and force your wife to feed them to try to make her marry one of them. She has refused, and she is wise, your Penelope. She told them that she could not marry again until she wove a shroud for your father Laertes so that he could be buried in honor. And the men granted her that. Each day she wove on it, and each night she unraveled it. But they have caught her in this trap and soon will force her to choose from among them."

"And what of my son?" asked Odysseus. "Does he sit idly by while all of this happens?"

"Your son is a fine man, and already he has made a long journey to search for you. But he has no one to help him and there are too many for him to fight alone. Already they have tried to kill him and only through my help did he escape."

"Then things are bad here," replied Odysseus. "But, come, you must have a plan. Tell me what I should do."

Athena, of course, did have a plan. So, following her suggestion, Odysseus went first to the home of his loyal swineherd, Eumaeus. There his son, Telemachus, was brought to him by Athena, and father and son were finally united.

Athena's plan for punishing the suitors called for Odysseus to undergo a lot of humiliation, for he was to dress as a beggar and return to his house. Odysseus was horrified when he arrived at his own house and saw over a hundred men lounging and carousing and flirting with his maidservants. They were all drunk, even though it was still day. When Odysseus arrived he was insulted and made fun of by everyone. No one followed the proper rules of courtesy to a beggar. One of the suitors, Antinoüs, even hit Odysseus with a stool.

At last the suitors returned home for the evening, and Penelope treated the stranger kindly, though without recognizing him, for Athena had disguised him and made him look much older than he really was.

The next day the suitors returned ready to kill and eat more of Odysseus' herd. On this day, at last, Penelope appeared before them and told them she had finally decided to marry one of them. But because she could not make up her mind, she had planned a contest.

"The task is quite simple," she said. "It is something that Odysseus used to do all of the time. I have here his own bow which he left behind when he went to war and a row of ax handles. The man who can string this bow and shoot an arrow through the ax handles, I will marry."

The men laughed at the challenge, and many were sure they would win, but they began to feel a little less sure when they saw the huge bow.

Telemachus immediately leaped and set up the axes in a long row, while the men handed the bow around. At last they were ready to try. But not a one of them was able to string the great bow. They even tried heating it to make it easier to bend, but none could bend it enough to string it.

In the meantime, Odysseus called out Eumaeus, the swineherd, and another faithful servant. He identified himself to them and proved his claim by showing them a scar on his leg which they both remembered. Then he told them to go through the hall and take out any weapons they found, and then he gave the signal to close and lock the doors to the hall.

He returned inside where the men were still struggling with the great bow. At last they gave it up and went back to their drinking. Odysseus asked if he could try to string the bow.

Antinoüs replied angrily, accusing the stranger of being drunk and threatening to send him off to a great ogre.

But Penelope intervened. "Antinoüs, you are showing neither good manners nor decency. I see no harm in letting the old fellow try to string the bow. Of course he won't try to marry me if he succeeds. If he succeeds, I will give him a new coat and tunic, which he sorely needs."

Then Telemachus spoke up, "Mother, I am tired of your having to put up with the insults of these men. I think you should go to your chamber and let me handle them." Penelope was surprised to see her son taking charge, but she was pleased, too, so she left.

In the meantime, Eumaeus had brought Odysseus the bow. The suitors continued to insult him as he turned the bow over in his hands. Then, almost before they knew what had happened, he strung the great bow effortlessly, and shot an arrow through the axes.

"Well, Telemachus," he said, "I did not disgrace you." And while the suitors still stood stunned, Telemachus grabbed a sword and spear and joined the stranger with the bow. Then Odysseus dropped off his rags and spread the arrows at his feet.

"That's one challenge won. Now I'll try another!" With that he shot an arrow straight at Antinoüs.

The suitors got up in anger and looked around frantically for their weapons and armor. "Stranger," they shouted, "you have gone too far. Now you will feel our anger."

"Dogs!" replied Odysseus. "You thought I would never return home. You thought you could rape my servants, harass my wife, and eat all my cattle and never pay for it. Now you will pay."

And so the fight began. Odysseus had three armed men, and the suitors, while they had no weapons, numbered over one hundred. But they were cowardly and, instead of rushing upon Odysseus all together, they tried to hide from the deadly arrows under the tables. Then Odysseus picked them off one by one.

But one of Odysseus' servants who had always disliked him managed to find some of the hidden weapons and gave them to the suitors. Now that some of the men had arms, the battle seemed bad for Odysseus. But then Mentor, an old man from the village, suddenly appeared. The suitors mocked him and threatened him, but Odysseus knew that it was Athena in disguise and that he could still win. However Athena did not join the fight. Instead she changed herself into a bird and watched from the rafters. But she still helped, for she caused all of the suitors to miss their mark. But when Odysseus and his three friends threw their lances, every one killed a man. Now they engaged in hand-to-hand combat with swords. And by the end of the fight, only two among the suitors remained alive, Phemius the minstrel and Medon the herald, who had only served the suitors unwillingly.

Then Odysseus called for Eurycleia, his old nurse, and asked her to send him all of his servants who had been unfaithful. These, too, he killed. Then the faithful servants came in and all wept to see their old master and rejoiced at the death of those who had oppressed them.

Last of all, Penelope herself came in. But she did not go directly to Odysseus to greet him. Too many times strangers had come pretending to be Odysseus. She only went over by the fireside and sat down, staring at the stranger. It had been twenty years since she had seen her husband. How could she know for sure if this was he?

Telemachus was angry. "Mother, how can you be so hard-hearted!" he cried. "You have waited all these years for Odysseus, and now you act as if you don't know him."

"I am numbed by the shock," she said quietly. "If it is really Odysseus, I will soon know."

Odysseus smiled. "Don't worry, son. Let your mother test me however she likes." So Odysseus went out and bathed and was dressed in a handsome tunic and cloak.

Then he returned and sat opposite his wife.

"You are surely an obstinate woman," he said. "Well, nurse, there is not much hope for it. Make me a bed outside in the hall."

"All right," said Penelope. "Eurycleia, take the big bed that is in my room and drag it outside into the hall."

"What!" cried Odysseus, forgetting that his wife was testing him. "Who has moved my bed! I built it myself and used for the bedpost a living olive tree that still hid its roots in the ground when I left it. Who has cut it down?"

Penelope's knees began to tremble, for she knew that no one but Odysseus could have known that secret, and she threw her arms around him and kissed him. Odysseus himself wept when he held his dear wife in his arms. And they went together to the great bed made with an olive tree which had waited for twenty years.

In many so-called primitive cultures it is a requirement of tribal initiation to spend a lengthy period alone in the forests or mountains, a period of coming to terms with the solitude and nonhumanity of nature so as to discover who, or what, one really is—a discovery hardly possible while the community is telling you what you are, or ought to be. He may discover, for instance, that loneliness is the masked fear of an unknown which is himself, and that the alien-looking aspect of nature is a projection upon the forests of his fear of stepping outside habitual and conditioned patterns of feeling.

ALAN W. WATTS

the oxherding pictures

The oxherding pictures of Zen Buddhism embody the quest of both the scamp and the dragon-slayer.

1. The search for the ox.
   The ox is not lost. It is man who has lost his spiritual power and knows that something is missing in his life.

2. Discovering the footprints.
   Now the man has discovered the right teachings, but he has not yet learned that the self and the external world are the same.

3. Finding the ox.
   Suddenly the man sees the ox and, seeing it, realizes that it is none other than himself.

4. Catching the ox.
   The man has caught a glimpse of the ox, but it requires constant discipline to bring it under control. He now has seen spiritual truth, but must continue working to be able to live constantly on a spiritual level.

226

5. Herding the ox.
    The man must be constantly alert or the ox, and his spiritual knowledge, will escape him.

6. Riding the ox.
    Now the ox and man are so disciplined that they function as one with no effort at all.

7. The ox is forgotten.
   Having attained this spiritual level, the ox is no longer needed and disappears, leaving the man to contemplate all of creation.

8. The ox and the man both transcended.
   At last, even the man himself is no longer needed and he has attained unity with the universe.

9. Reaching the source.

Now the man can sit in serenity and watch the plan and growth of the world, being totally unaffected by it. He now carries the sack of blessings which he can bestow on mankind.

10. Living in the world.

The man now returns to the world, living his life in simplicity and harmony. He is in the world, but not of the world.

CAN MEN LIVE TOGETHER IN PEACE?

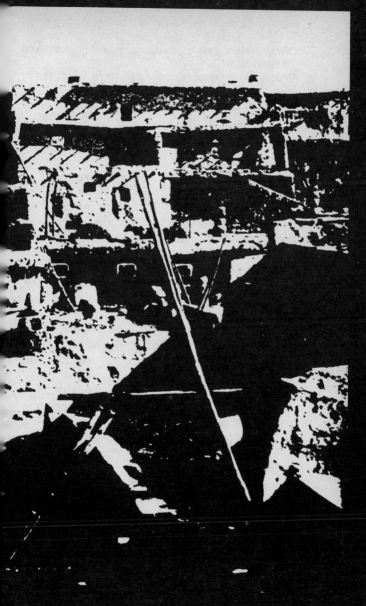

People have never liked to live alone.
But they have usually had a hard time living together.

Laws, armies, social customs, governments, and
  kings
All seem to be necessary for people to live together
  in peace.

If these do not exist
Revenge becomes the law
And the strongest—or the cleverest—wins.

medea's revenge

GREEK

Medea was almost out of her mind with grief and despair. Her husband, Jason, had just deserted her to marry King Creon's daughter, and Creon had followed this insult by banishing Medea and her two sons from the country. There was no way that a single woman with two sons could support herself honorably in ancient Greece. And Medea could never return to her homeland. Medea wept even more at the thought of her father and the way she had tricked him to save Jason.

Medea remembered that day so long ago when Jason, a handsome young prince, had come sailing up in his fine ship, the *Argo*. He had come, he said, in quest of the golden fleece which had been brought to Asia Minor by a relative of his, and he must recover it, he continued, to regain the throne of his country.

The story now seemed terribly ironic, for Jason's relative, who had arrived in Asia Minor riding on the golden ram, had been disowned by his father just as Jason was now disowning his own children.

But then Medea had been young and romantic and easily impressed by the handsome and bold stranger from the exciting land of Greece. As Jason told of the adventures that he and his Argonauts had experienced, Medea fell in love with him. However, Medea's father, King Aetes, was much less impressed with the haughty and opportunistic Jason and said that he would give him the golden fleece only if he could perform two almost impossible tasks.

"You must take two powerful bulls that breathe fire and yoke them to a plow. Then you are to plow a field and sow it with dragons' teeth." Jason had only laughed at these tasks, but Medea shuddered, for she knew the strength of the bulls, and even worse, she knew that as soon as the dragons' teeth were sown into the field, they would turn into armed men who would turn on Jason and destroy him.

So that night she had slipped into Jason's quarters and offered her help, for Medea was skilled in witchcraft and was a favorite of the goddess Hecate. Jason had promised before the altar of Hecate to marry Medea for her favors, and Medea had given him two charms. One made him invincible for a whole day and the other caused the men who sprang from

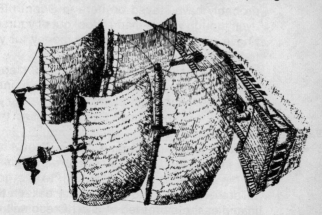

the dragons' teeth to fight among themselves and kill each other off.

With Medea's charms, Jason had succeeded in his quest and fled immediately with the fleece and Medea, for King Aetes was not willing to give up either the fleece or his daughter gracefully.

Medea shuddered in memory of that flight, for she had committed a horrible crime to save Jason. Seeing her father following them, she had taken her brother with her, and as her father and his army approached, she had killed him and cut his body into pieces. Then she had thrown the pieces of his body into the ocean, and her despairing father had given up the chase to find the remains of his son's body so he could give him a proper burial.

All this Medea had done for Jason, and now he was deserting her. In the middle of her rage and anger, a servant announced that Jason was coming to her room.

Jason walked in with infuriating calm. "Well, my little witch," he taunted. "Your nasty temper has caused you trouble again. If you hadn't made such a fuss about all of this, you could probably have stayed on here in Corinth. But even though you've made a fool out of yourself, I have come to offer you some money for you to use in exile."

"You beastly coward!" screamed Medea. "Do you think you can buy me off with money? What has happened to all of the vows you made before the gods? Don't you fear their vengeance?"

"Now, Medea," laughed Jason, "you know that in this world a man has to protect himself by his own might. You may look to the gods to protect you if you wish. But I believe that marrying the daughter of King Creon will get me further than all of your sacrifices to Hecate. A man by himself is weak, but allied with a powerful king, he is strong."

"Get out of here," Medea cried in fury. "It is bad enough that you are deserting me, without gloating over my downfall."

But as soon as he was gone, Medea thought over his words. "He is right," she thought. "The weak in this world are lost. A man, and even more a woman, must be strong and avenge evil against herself or she will be destroyed. I must avenge myself, and Jason—of all people—should know that I have the power to do it."

Back to her magic arts Medea went, and when everything was ready, she called for Jason again. This time she appeared contrite and calm.

"I have been foolish, Jason," she said. "I know that it is too late for me to escape being sent into exile, but I hope that perhaps your new wife will have pity on our sons and let them stay. I have prepared a great wedding gift for her and hope that if our boys take it to her she will have pity on them." With that, Medea called her two sons to come out with a marvelous cloak and a gold crown and sent them to the princess with Jason.

Medea waited eagerly and soon the children returned with the happy news that the princess had indeed agreed that they could stay. Medea hardly listened to their words for she was listening for something else, and soon she heard it—a scream of anguish and then a loud wailing. Soon a messenger came running with a look of horror on his face.

"Fly, Medea," he cried. "You have done the most horrible deed in the world. Get out while you still can!"

"Tell me what you saw," Medea begged.

"It was horrible!" gasped the messenger. "The bride was delighted with the beautiful robe and the golden crown and eagerly put them on. But suddenly her face turned pale, and she gasped in pain. And as we watched in horror, the diadem and the robe burst into flame and burned her entire body as she screamed in pain. Then Creon rushed in and, before anyone could stop him, he had taken

her into his arms and was also engulfed in flames. And he, too, died a horrible and painful death!''

"And thus be it done to all of the enemies of Medea," the sorceress shouted triumphantly.

Then with an even more dreadful look, Medea took her two sons into the chamber and stabbed them both. "Poor babes," she moaned in anguish. "It is better for you to die by your mother's hand than to remain here and be mistreated by your enemies all of your lives."

Jason arrived to see Medea carrying their bodies to a magical chariot drawn by fierce black dragons. Before he could reach them, Medea and his dead sons were gone and he knew he would never see them again.

Crushed by grief, Jason left Corinth and wandered throughout Greece. Seeking relief in his old glories, Jason went down to his famous ship, the *Argo*, which was now old and rotting. As he stepped upon its deck, the old ship broke in two, falling on its old master and killing him.

Where there is no law, the weak must protect themselves by any means they can discover.

signy's, siggeir's, andvari's, sigmund's, regin's, brynhild's, sigund's REVENGE

There was a great wedding feast in the hall of the Volsungs, for Signy, the daughter of Volsung, king of the Huns, was to be married. Into the midst of the festivities came a strange old man with one eye and a blue-gray cloak, who immediately commanded the attention of everyone in the hall. For it was in this guise that Odin himself appeared in the land of man.

"Lords of the Goths and Volsungs," he cried. "I bring you here a gift." And throwing back his cloak he revealed a marvelous sword. While all of the wedding guests stared, he thrust it deep into the trunk of a tree. "This sword is to be the prize of the strongest man in the world."

All the men at the feast tried their luck, but none could budge the great sword, until at last, Sigmund, the eldest son of Volsung, pulled it out with no effort.

Humiliated by Sigmund's success, Siggeir, the groom of Signy, later invited King Volsung and his sons to the land of the Goths where he killed them all, leaving them to be devoured by a wolf. But Sigmund, with the help of his sister Signy, escaped and hid near the castle. Signy had a son by her brother Sigmund whom she named Sinfiotli, and he and his father eventually attacked the castle of Siggeir. They killed him and all of his children and burned the castle, and Signy watched her revenge on her husband grimly. But at the last minute, she left her conquering brother and son and returned to the burning castle to die with her husband.

Sigmund returned to the home of the Volsungs where he hoped to rule in peace, but his first wife poisoned his son, Sinfiotli. His second wife, Hiordis, was faithful, but shortly after his marriage to her Sigmund was killed by Odin because the sword he had drawn from the tree made him invincible by any mortal and the gods feared he would become too powerful. After his death, his wife had a son whom she named Sigurd, or in the German version, Siegfried.

Many years earlier events took place which were to have an influence on Sigurd's life. Long ago there had been a dwarf named Rodmar who had three sons, Otter, Regin, and Fafnir, who had the power to change themselves into animals. One day while Otter was in the form of an otter, he was killed by Loki who was traveling with Odin and Hoenir, two other gods. Not knowing that they

had killed Rodmar's son, they arrived at his house with the skin. Rodmar, of course, recognized his son, even in disguise, and said that he would kill the three gods unless they covered the entire body with gold.

Loki the mischief maker found Andvari, a dwarf who had a tremendous hoard of gold including a magic ring whose touch bred gold. The dwarf was helpless against Loki's superior power and made little protest when Loki took the gold, but when he also demanded the ring, Andvari became so angry that he cursed the ring.

"Whoever wears this ring will receive nothing but sorrows from it," he shouted.

Loki returned with the gold and ransomed the gods. He intended to keep the ring, but Rodmar found one spot of Otter's body which was not covered, and Loki was forced to yield the ring also. Rodmar eagerly put on the ring and began to admire his treasure.

But the curses of the ring went to work quickly. That night Fafnir sneaked into his father's room and killed him, and turned himself into a dragon to guard his treasure.

Regin fled in terror and eventually came to the land where Hiordis lived with her young son Sigurd. Immediately foreseeing Sigurd's great strength, Regin began to plan his revenge on Fafnir. He offered himself to young Sigurd as a tutor, for he knew the art of blacksmithing as well as the secrets of the runes and other mysteries of the gods.

When Sigurd was grown, Regin began to forge a sword for him. When it was complete, he gave it to the young man, but Sigurd brought it down on the anvil with one fierce blow and it shattered to bits. Regin went back to work and forged a new sword, but Sigurd broke it just as quickly. At last Hiordis brought out the remains of Sigmund's great sword which had been broken by Odin at his death.

Regin was afraid of this metal of the gods, but he was so eager to kill his brother and obtain the gold for himself that he forged the sword and gave it to Sigurd. This time Sigurd smote the anvil with a mighty blow and split the anvil in two. Then Regin told him of Fafnir and the gold, and Sigurd was eager to try his new sword on this beast. But before going Sigurd had one more need. Out in the pastures he found a great horse named Greyfell, a descendant of Sleipnir, Odin's own horse. He asked the king for this mount and was given it.

Now Sigurd and Regin set off for the dragon Fafnir. "You must smite him in the belly," Regin said. "And after you have killed him, you may

have all the gold, but you must give me Fafnir's heart to eat, for that way I will obtain all of his knowledge.''

When they arrived at Fafnir's house, they saw a much-used trail leading from the house to the river. Sigurd dug a hole in the middle of this trail and concealed himself in it so he could strike the dragon in his vulnerable stomach. The next morning Sigurd heard the great dragon coming along the path and soon everything turned black as the dragon glided over his hole. When he judged that the heart was right over him, Sigurd gave a mighty stroke with his sword and pierced the dragon's heart. In his death pangs the mighty dragon thrashed about, but Sigurd was safe in his hole.

When the dragon was dead, he stepped out and cut out the heart as Regin had bidden him to. But while he was roasting it, he touched it to see if it was done. The blood sizzled out and burned his hand, and Sigurd quickly put his hand into his mouth. As soon as he tasted Fafnir's blood, he could understand the speech of the birds above him.

"Beware, Sigurd," he heard the birds say. "Regin will try to kill you so he can have the gold for himself."

Sure enough, Regin soon came bearing a cup of poisoned wine. But warned by the birds, Sigurd threw the cup down and killed Regin with a stroke of his sword.

Wearing Andvari's ring, Sigurd set out for his next adventure. This, too, resulted from actions of the gods.

Brynhild was one of the Valkyrie, the maidens of Odin who chose the best of the slain warriors and carried them to Valhalla. But one day in battle she fell in love with one of the men who was fated to die and spared him, taking a man whose death was not foreordained instead. For this act of disobedience she was banished from the gods and turned into a mortal maiden. At her request, however, Odin placed her within a circle of fire which only the bravest of mortal men could penetrate.

So as he traveled up a strange mountain, Sigurd saw a great ring of fire. Seeing a chance for a great adventure, Sigurd spurred his great horse Greyfell and broke through the ring of fire. Inside he saw what appeared to be the body of a warrior on a funeral pyre. But when Sigurd took the helmet off the body, he found that it was actually a beautiful woman, and that she was alive. Then with his great sword, he slit her armor. Slowly her eyes opened and she smiled at him.

For several days they stayed in seclusion on

the mountain top. But eventually Brynhild said that she must return to the land of mortals and Sigurd also must return to his home. But before they parted, Sigurd gave Brynhild the ring and promised to return for her as soon as he had a kingdom worthy of her.

As he was traveling, Sigurd came to the land of the Nibelung. He was welcomed by the king Guiki and his wife, Grimhild, and his sons Gunnar, Hogni, and Guttorm. Their sister Gudrun immediately fell in love with the handsome stranger.

The queen Grimhild saw that Gudrun was in love with Sigurd and thought that he would make an excellent husband for her. But Sigurd payed no attention to Gudrun, and Grimhild wisely assumed that Sigurd was already in love with some other lady. Grimhild, though, was a clever magician and mixed a potion which would make Sigurd forget any other woman he loved.

One night while the warriors were all singing, Grimhild herself brought him the charm. Immediately he completely forgot all about Brynhild and fell madly in love with Gudrun.

Sigurd asked Guiki for the hand of Gudrun, who agreed on the condition that Sigurd would help his son Gunnar win the fair Brynhild, whose fame had already spread throughout the land. Sigurd, who did not ever remember having heard the name before, willingly agreed.

But when Sigurd and Gunnar along with many friends went to woo Brynhild they found her again surrounded by flames. Gunnar tried in vain to ride through them but failed. So by means of a charm provided by his mother, Gunnar changed Sigurd into his own form and Sigurd successfully rode through the flames. When he succeeded in entering, Brynhild as-

sumed that Sigurd must be dead, for as long
as he was alive, no one else could have pene-
trated the flames. So she gave the man she
supposed to be Gunnar the ring which Sigurd
had given to her. Even this did not awaken
Sigurd's memory.

So Brynhild came to the palace of the Nibelungs to marry Gunnar. But by the time she
arrived, the charm of Grimhild had worn off
and Sigurd recognized her. Then both Sigurd
and Brynhild knew that they had been trapped.
Both made the best of things and tried to enjoy
their wedded spouses, but in Brynhild's heart

love and hate for Sigurd alternated and smoldered.

At last one day she and Gudrun quarreled over whose husband was the greatest. Brynhild insisted that since Gunnar had ridden through the ring of fire, he was the greatest hero alive. But Gudrun, who knew the true story, told her that it had really been Sigurd disguised as Gunnar. As proof, she showed Brynhild the ring which Sigurd had given to her.

Mad with rage, Brynhild plotted Sigurd's death. She chose Guttorm, the brother of Gunnar, to perform the deed. And that night, when Sigurd was asleep, he slipped into the chamber and stabbed him. With his dying effort, Sigurd threw his sword after Guttorm and killed him.

A great funeral pyre was built for Sigurd, and as the flames reached skyward, Brynhild rushed into their midst and died with her beloved Sigurd.

The curse of the ring now fell on Gudrun and brought the end of the house of Nibelung. The treasure and the ring were finally lost at the bottom of the Rhine.

What do I care about the law.
Ain't I got the power?

Cornelius Vanderbilt

MYTH, MUSIC, AND NATIONALISM

The story of Sigurd, who in Germany was known as Siegfried, became one of the most powerful influences on German thought, and particularly the composer Richard Wagner. He retold the story, with many variations, in a grand cycle of four operas called the Ring of the Niebelungen. In Wagner's version, the ring is even more powerful and eventually brings about the death of the gods themselves and the burning of Valhalla.

"Whoever wants to understand National Socialist Germany must know Wagner," Hitler used to say.

It was not his political writings, however, but his towering operas, recalling so vividly the world of German antiquity with its heroic myths, its fighting pagan gods and heroes, its demons and dragons, its blood feuds and primitive tribal codes, its sense of destiny, of the splendor of love and life and the nobility of death which inspired the myths of modern Germany and gave it a Germanic *Weltanschauung* which Hitler and the Nazis, with some justification, took over as their own. . . .

Siegfried and Kriemhild, Brunhild and Hagen—these are the ancient heroes and heroines with whom so many modern Germans liked to identify themselves. With them and with the world of the barbaric, pagan Nibelungs—an irrational, heroic, mystic world, beset by

249

treachery, overwhelmed by violence, drowned in blood, and culminating in the *Goetterdaemmerung,* the twilight of the gods, as Valhalla, set on flames by Wotan after all his vicissitudes, goes up in flames in an orgy of self-willed annihilation which has always fascinated the German mind and answered some terrible longing in the German soul. These heroes, this primitive, demonic world, were always, in Mell's words, "in the people's soul." In that German soul could be felt the struggle between the spirit of civilization and the spirit of the Nibelungs, and in the time with which this history is concerned the latter seemed to gain the upper hand. It is not at all surprising that Hitler tried to emulate Wotan when in 1945 he willed the destruction of Germany so that it might go down in flames with him.

From *The Rise and Fall of the Third Reich*

> It is not right to say that when man has no law or law enforcers he resorts to the law of the jungle, for no jungle animals live by the law of revenge.

revenge in zen

There was once a samurai who fell in love with his master's wife. So he killed the master and ran away with his wife, but she was so greedy that he soon left her.

Then the samurai began to feel guilty and decided that he must do a good deed to atone for his sins. As he was traveling along he came to a very steep road over a mountain and discovered that many people had been killed trying to cross it. So he decided to build a tunnel through the mountain.

He had been working for a year when the son of the master whom he had killed appeared and threatened to cut off his head.

"You have a right to kill me," said the samurai. "But could you please wait until I finish this tunnel?"

The young man agreed, and after watching for several weeks he began to work with his old enemy. Finally, after several more months, the tunnel was completed and people could walk safely through the mountain.

"Now you may kill me," said the samurai.

"How can I kill you now?" said the young man. "You are my own teacher."

cheyenne council of 44

"In the old days," say the Cheyenne, "there were no laws. People did what they wanted to."

Many years ago an old man killed his wife and abandoned his children. When the children finally caught up with the camp, their father dragged them through the village, saying, "I am going to punish these children of mine

252

because they killed their mother and ate her.''

The people believed him and would not listen
to the children, so they helped the father tie
his children to stakes in the ground and left
them to starve. Then they moved.

But as soon as the people had gone, a large
black dog came to the two children, chewed
the ropes loose and freed them. Then a voice
said, ''There is a wikiup over there. Go to it.''

When the children looked up, they found the
wikiup with a bear and a lion living in it. The
children were frightened, but they obeyed the
words of the voice and moved in.

Then they heard the voice say, "Look at the buffalo."

The girl looked at the buffalo and discovered that she had wonderful medicine powers, for all the buffalo fell dead before her eyes.

The girl and her brother eagerly butchered one of the animals and the girl sent a crow with some of the buffalo fat back to the people of her tribe, who quickly returned, for they had found no food.

The first person to visit them was the children's father. As soon as he came into the lodge, the bear and the lion, who had been kind to the children, killed him and ate him.

Then the girl sent for all the men and women in the tribe. "We are going to make chiefs and set up laws," she announced. "My brother and I were treated unjustly because you had no laws. Now we will make a rule that if someone kills a fellow tribesman he must be banished for from one to five years."

Then she gave to the people a ceremony for the choosing of chiefs. She set up a special lodge and took a pipe. She chose five head chiefs and made them swear to be honest and take care of the tribe.

She then gave the people other sacred objects and taught them special ceremonies. "Every ten years," she told them, "you must choose new chiefs and have a renewal ceremony, but you must keep five of the old ones."

"From now on," she said, "the Cheyenne will be a great people, for we will live together with just laws and good chiefs."

❝ We, like the eagles, were born to be free. Yet we are obliged, in order to live at all, to make a cage of laws for ourselves and to stand on the perch. ❞

WILLIAM BOLITHO

In ancient, barbaric Greece, justice was of little use against armed might. What justice there was depended upon the gods who were usually so involved in their own intrigues that they had little time to be concerned with the behavior of men. Often punishments were delayed so long that they fell on the grandchildren instead of the sinner himself. So it was in the case of Atreus.

Atreus himself committed one of the most heinous crimes in history. His brother Thyestes fell in love with Atreus' wife, and in revenge, Atreus killed Thyestes' son and served the corpse for supper. Thyestes, having no power himself to avenge his son, called upon the gods to curse the house of Atreus.

This horrible deed probably reminded the gods of another crime committed by an ancestor of Atreus, Tantalus. *(Tantalize:* to tempt with something unattainable.) He lived in the days when the gods walked the earth with men; he tried to prove the stupidity of the gods by cutting up his own son Pelops and serving him to the gods for a meal. The gods, however, were not stupid and brought the boy back to life. Tantalus was sent to a pool in Hades where they tortured him by standing him up to his neck in water with delicious fruits hanging over his head. Whenever he stooped to drink, the water receded, and whenever he reached up to pluck the fruits, they were whisked up beyond his reach.

Atreus should have learned from this punishment of his ancestor, but he did not. However, the gods did not get around to punishing

the house of atreus

Atreus, but left the vengeance to fall on his two sons, Menelaus and Agamemnon. Perhaps the whole Trojan War could be considered part of the punishment to the house of Atreus because it was Menelaus' wife who became Helen of Troy. But the bulk of the evil fell on Agamemnon and his family.

In order to sail to Troy, Agamemnon was told that he must sacrifice his daughter Iphigenia. Clytemnestra, Agamemnon's wife, was furious when Agamemnon agreed, and she refused to remain faithful to a husband who would kill his own daughter for the sake of glory. So she took as a lover one of Agamemnon's enemies, Aegisthus, a descendant of Thyestes whom Agamemnon's father had so mistreated.

Clytemnestra's hatred against Agamemnon increased as the stories of his love affairs at Troy came back. To make matters worse, when Agamemnon returned to his home after the war was over, he brought with him a new woman, Cassandra, the daughter of Priam, king of Troy.

Cassandra was a prophetess and as soon as she set foot in Mycenae, Agamemnon's home, she fell into a trance and began to prophesy death for Agamemnon and herself. The townspeople watched with foreboding as Agamemnon approached his palace where Clytemnestra and Aegisthus waited for him. The great doors were shut and a loud scream was heard. Then Clytemnestra opened the doors to reveal the body of her husband.

"Iphigenia is now avenged!" she cried.

But this was only the beginning of the bloody vengeance, for her other daughter, Elektra, felt stronger ties to her father than to her sister and she was determined that her father's death would not go unavenged. Fearing her mother's crazed state and Aegisthus' ambition, she took

256

her young brother, Orestes, and fled with him to another country where she gave him to friends to raise. Then she returned home.

Many years later, Orestes was grown and returned to his home with his friend Pylades. Not knowing what he would find there, he came as a stranger, and, instead of going to the palace, went to the graveyard to weep on the grave of his father.

There Elektra found him. Together they plotted. They were determined to kill Aegisthus to avenge their father, but could they kill their mother, too? Was not the crime of parricide worse than allowing their father's death to go unavenged? Unable to decide for himself, Orestes had gone to the oracle of Apollo. The answer was clear: Clytemnestra must be killed.

Their plan was simple. Pylades and Orestes were to go to the palace disguised as strangers bringing the message that Orestes had died. As they had planned, Clytemnestra invited them in, and once inside the palace, Orestes revealed who he was and immediately killed Aegisthus.

But Clytemnestra pleaded, "How can you kill your own mother? I brought you into this world. You nursed at my breast."

Orestes almost gave in to her pleading. "She is right, Pylades. I cannot kill my own mother."

"Do you dare disobey Apollo's oracle?" asked Pylades.

"You're right," Orestes replied, and with one stroke of his sword, he killed her. But immediately a change came over him. An unseen horror seemed to haunt him.

"Look," he screamed. "Can't you see them? Those dreadful women with blood dripping from their eyes!" Orestes waved his sword madly at the creatures that were haunting him.

257

But with no effect. At last he turned to flee them.

Elektra caught him and tried to hold him, "It is only your imagination," she pleaded. "Come in and rest and this horrible vision will go away."

But Orestes rushed out of her sight. For years he traveled from one land to another driven onward by the horrible Furies. For that is who they were, the terrible goddesses with snakes for hair who had sprung up from the blood of ancient Uranus and who were destined to remain on earth until all injustice disappeared.

So the cycle of revenge continued with the Furies avenging Clytemnestra, who had no one else to plead for her. But at last Apollo felt that Orestes' punishment was sufficient and he ordered him to go to Athens where Athena could cleanse him of his sin.

There in Athens was held perhaps the first trial by jury in the history of the world. Athena refused to make the decision but called the wise men of Athens together. Apollo himself pleaded the case for Orestes, and the Furies argued eloquently against him.

The question was so difficult that the jury was evenly divided and Athena herself had to cast the deciding vote—for acquittal. Orestes was free.

But Athena could not disregard the proper wrath of the Furies, so she invited them to stay in Athens, promising them a home and worship worthy of them. They accepted her invitation and from then on have been called the Eumenides, the Benevolent Ones, and instead of punishing the guilty, they now plead the cases of the weak and poor.

Whether there really was a Camelot or not, it has come to symbolize for the English what Athens symbolized for the Greeks, an ancient, beautiful time when justice and reason ruled humanity.

arthur:
might for right

It all began with Merlin, that strange wizard from the enchanted forest who taught Arthur the secrets of the world and then succumbed to a woman's charms.

Out of the ancient, pre-Christian mysteries of druids and fairies, the dark shadow of an incubus floated one night over a virgin princess and impregnated her.

Cast into a dungeon, the poor girl bemoaned her fate, and there in the darkness, Merlin was born. Immediately he could talk and told his mother not to be upset, for he was destined to greatness. But his mother feared his supernatural origin and sent for a priest to baptize her fairy child. As the holy water dropped on his head, the demonic portion of his origin was tamed, but many of his supernatural powers remained.

It happened that in that country, the king Vortigern was trying to build a great castle, but each time he built it, the castle fell down. Being told by an astrologer that he must sacrifice a babe with no human father on the foundation, Vortigern sent for Merlin. Merlin was torn from his weeping mother and went boldly with Vortigern's men. When the infant was brought before the king, he sat up and began to speak.

Vortigern and his court stared in amazement as the babe told them that the real problem of the castle was that Vortigern was trying to build it over a cave in which two dragons were fighting.

261

Sure enough, when Vortigern's men dug up the foundation, a red dragon and a white dragon were found in combat, and as the court watched, the white dragon killed the red one.

"The red dragon is you, Vortigern," said the infant Merlin. "The white dragon is the rightful heirs to the throne, Uther and Pendragon, who will soon return to claim their heritage."

It happened as Merlin had prophesied, for soon the two brothers came with a great army and overthrew Vortigern, who was burned alive in his own castle. Merlin became the chief adviser of Pendragon and his brother Uther, who became king when Pendragon died.

But even while he was advising the two kings on the affairs of state and entertaining the court with his magic powers, Merlin was preparing the way for a greater king to come. King Uther fell in love with a beautiful lady named Igraine and begged Merlin to woo her for him.

"I will win the Lady Igraine for your wife," replied Merlin, "if you will promise to give me your first son to raise."

So it was that Arthur was carried away from the palace of his father and brought up by the enchanter Merlin. In the castle of Sir Ector, far from London, Merlin taught the young boy the wisdom of the ancients and the skills of animals. He instilled in him the virtues of chivalry and prepared him for his duties as king.

At last King Uther died and the nobles gathered together to elect a new king. It promised to be a bloody struggle, for none knew that the king had a son and many wanted the throne for themselves. On Christmas Day all were gathered together in the church to pray when suddenly a great stone appeared in the churchyard with a large sword in it. An inscription in gold was written above the sword which.

read: "Whoever pulls this sword from this stone is the rightful king of all of England."

All of the nobles tried for the sword but none was successful. At last the archbishop decreed that upon New Year's Day another trial would be made and all the knights of England would be invited.

In the meantime Sir Kay, the son of Sir Ector, went to a great tournament and young Arthur went as his squire. On the way they passed the sword in the stone but did not try their strength. But when they arrived at the tournament, Sir Kay discovered that he had left his sword at home.

"Return with haste and get my sword," said Sir Kay to Arthur, who quickly mounted his horse and started on the long ride. While he was riding he again saw the sword in the stone and decided that he could certainly bring this sword more quickly than he could return home.

So he dismounted and walked up to the stone. Not bothering to read the inscription, he slipped the sword out of the stone and rode back to Sir Kay.

When he arrived he gave the sword to Sir Kay who looked at it in amazement. Sir Kay took it to his father who was also amazed, and before Arthur's startled eyes, both bowed down in front of him and hailed him as their king.

On Twelfth Day all of the knights assembled again by the stone and this time Arthur was there, too. When all of them had tried again and failed, they were annoyed to see a fifteen-year-old boy walk up to the sword. And when he easily drew the sword from the stone they became furious. "We do not want a mere boy to be our king," they all agreed and decided to try the contest at Candlemas. But at Candlemas, and again at Easter, the same thing happened.

Now Sir Ector went to the Archbishop of Canterbury who drew all of King Uther's special knights to Arthur's side. He also invited the common people of the land to the next trial which would be held at Pentecost. This time when Arthur drew out the sword, all of the people shouted, "Arthur is our king, for it is God's will." Then all of the nobles knelt before him and Arthur was proclaimed king.

However, not all of the lords were willing to call Arthur king, and Arthur was forced to fight many battles to keep the kingdom together. After these wars were over, King Arthur visited King Lot and fell in love with his wife, Morgana, who was the mother of Gawaine, Gaheris, Agravain, and Gareth, who would later be among Arthur's greatest knights. But more important, she was Arthur's own sister, for she was the daughter of Igraine by her first husband. But Arthur did not yet know his parentage, and, as if already preparing for his downfall, he had a son by Morgana and named him Mordred.

It was only then that Merlin revealed Arthur's birth, and Arthur was very upset that he had unknowingly had a child by his sister.

"Your doom will come when it is time," Merlin warned him, "but there is no benefit in worrying about it now. You have great deeds to perform before then."

Arthur decided that he had better marry properly before he made another horrible mistake with women, so he went to Merlin for advice.

"Is there a lady that you have in mind?" Merlin asked.

"Yes," replied Arthur. "While returning from the wars, I stopped at the castle of King Leode-

grance who had a very beautiful daughter named Guinevere. He must have been a good friend of my father because he showed me a great Round Table which my father King Uther gave him as a gift."

"I fear that prophecies of ill are coming true, for I know that this woman, too, will bring great evil to your court," said Merlin thoughtfully, "but it cannot be helped, so I will assist you in winning her."

So Merlin took Arthur and a group of knights, all disguised, to the castle of King Leodegrance. When they arrived, they found that he was besieged by an enemy from Ireland. The next day when the enemy attacked, Arthur and his men took arms and went to the gates of the castle, but the porter refused to open for anyone but the king, so Merlin opened the gates by magic.

Arthur and his knights were greatly outnumbered, but Merlin caused a fog to cover the battlefield so that the enemy could not see how few they were. However, Merlin made a hole in the fog where Arthur was so that Guinevere, who was watching from the ramparts, could see his exploits. She watched him kill many of the enemy, including a huge giant fifteen feet high.

When they returned to the castle to the grateful Leodegrance and the admiring Guinevere, Merlin explained that the purpose of their mission was to secure a bride for their leader, and Leodegrance willingly gave Guinevere to the strange knight without even knowing his name. When Leodegrance found that his new son-in-law was Arthur, king of England and his own lord, he was so thrilled that he gave the couple the great Round Table as a wedding gift.

So Arthur and Guinevere returned to Camelot where a great celebration was held, and he sent out a call to all the knights of the world to come to his court and be seated at the great Round Table. All who came were required to prove their bravery and nobility by undertaking great feats of strength and by taking an oath each Pentecost swearing never to do outrage or murder, to give help to ladies and damsels, and never to do battle for a wrongful quarrel.

Soon knights came from all over the country. Arthur's four nephews, Gawaine, Gaheris, Agravain, and Gareth, were among those chosen as knights of the Round Table. The knights went forth on great adventures and Arthur also led them to battles in Norway and France. Many of their adventures, however, were planned by Merlin to continually force them to remember their chivalrous oath.

In the midst of an enchanted forest in a mirage-lake lived a nymph named Viviane, also known as the Lady of the Lake. It was from this nymph that Arthur received his sword Excalibur, and later his greatest knight, Lancelot. Lancelot, the son of King Ban of Brittany, was taken when an infant by the Lady of the Lake and raised in her castle with his cousins Lionel and Bohort.

When Lancelot was of age, he was sent to the court of King Arthur where he quickly became known as the most powerful knight in the court. None could vanquish him. But as soon as he appeared, Queen Guinevere fell in love with him and he with her.

And at this time the Lady of the Lake caused another terrible blow to Arthur's court, for she had fallen in love with Merlin and he with her. At her request he had taught her all of his magic and she had used it to imprison him in a tower forever.

So Merlin disappeared from Arthur's court forever. The only word that was heard from him was heard by Sir Gawaine as he once wandered lost in the enchanted forest.

"Sir Gawaine, Sir Gawaine," he heard a voice say. "It is I, Merlin. I have been imprisoned forever by my beautiful nymph and can no more return to Arthur's court. But he has learned my lessons well and no longer needs me. Only one more piece of advice do I have to give you. All of the knights of the Round Table must go on the quest for the Holy Grail."

Sir Gawaine returned to the court with the message and the quest was eagerly taken up by all of the knights. The quest was gloriously fulfilled by Sir Galahad, but it brought disaster to the Round Table, for many of the knights who went on the quest did not return.

One day a strange, sinister-looking lad appeared at the court. "I am Mordred," he announced, and Arthur's heart trembled. For Mordred was his own son by his sister and he remembered Merlin's prophecy that Mordred would bring about the destruction of his realm. But he tried to do his best for his son and trusted him with his kingdom.

When the knights returned from the quest for the Grail, Sir Mordred discovered Sir Lancelot's love for Guinevere and began to plot his fall. Mordred boldly confronted King Arthur with the unfaithfulness of his queen, and demanded that Arthur test her by going on a hunting trip and not taking Lancelot.

Just as Mordred had planned, Lancelot came to the queen's chamber shortly after Arthur left. Then Mordred, Agravain, and twelve other knights burst in on them. "Traitor!" they shouted. Lancelot started up with his sword and with his great might fought them off and escaped.

But the knights bound Guinevere and took her before Arthur, demanding her death.

"Alas," moaned Arthur. "The fellowship of the Round Table is now broken forever, and I cannot by law let the queen live." So Guinevere was sentenced to burn at the stake.

The day of her execution she was led out by a priest and tied to a great stake around which were piled masses of wood. Suddenly the sound of hoofbeats was heard and Sir Lancelot galloped up with his men. Lancelot cut the ropes that bound Guinevere and put her on his horse. Arthur's knights tried to bar his way, even though they were unarmed. Lancelot ruthlessly cut his way through them, killing Gareth and Geharis, the brothers of Sir Gawaine, and the nephews of the king. Then Sir Gawaine rushed to the king and swore to fight Lancelot to the death.

It was a sad army that set out to fight Lancelot and an even sadder group that gathered in Lancelot's castle. For they were fighting against their old friends, and no matter what happened, there was no way for the battle to end happily. Lancelot was the most unhappy of all, and once in battle saved the king's life and knelt on the battlefield begging forgiveness.

The Pope himself was disturbed when news of this war reached him, and he ordered Lancelot to give Guinevere back to the king and ordered Arthur to make peace with Lancelot. Both willingly obeyed his orders, and Arthur returned to Camelot and Lancelot returned to his ancestral lands in France.

But Sir Gawaine would not give up the fight against the man who had killed his two brothers, and he finally persuaded Arthur to attack Lancelot in his homeland. Very reluctantly, Arthur agreed, and leaving Guinevere and his kingdom in the care of Mordred, he set sail for France.

This was the chance Mordred had been waiting for. He forged letters from France saying that Arthur was dead and made arrangements to have himself crowned and to marry Guinevere. But Guinevere was not about to marry Mordred. She fled to London and locked herself in the tower, threatening to kill herself if Mordred pursued.

Arthur and Sir Gawaine returned immediately to England, but not before Sir Gawaine had been mortally wounded by Lancelot. Mordred met them at Dover with a great army, but Arthur's knights fought so bravely that they were able to land. As they were burying the dead knights, King Arthur came upon Sir Gawaine, who was dying.

"I am dying of the wound from Sir Lancelot," he said. "So now our quarrel is over. Send for Lancelot now, for he will come and fight against Mordred with you." Then he died.

The battle continued for several weeks. But one night Sir Gawaine appeared to Arthur in a dream. "Do not go against Sir Mordred tomorrow or you will be killed," he warned.

King Arthur heeded the dream and sent two of his bishops to make a temporary truce with Mordred. They were more successful than they had hoped, for Mordred agreed to stop the war if he were given Cornwall and Kent and named Arthur's heir.

So Arthur agreed to meet Mordred between the two armies to make the truce. Both parties were very wary, for neither trusted the other. But evil still waited for Arthur, for one of the

knights was stung by an adder and drew his sword to kill it. The other knights, thinking he meant to betray the truce, drew their swords and the battle began anew.

So Arthur and Mordred faced each other upon the battlefield. Arthur took his spear in both hands and ran it clear through his traitorous son. But Mordred clasped his sword, and with his last strength, smote Arthur on the head with such a blow that it split his helmet and his skull.

Sir Bedivere carried Arthur from the field and laid him in a quiet spot.

"My time has come," Arthur whispered. "Take my sword and throw it in the lake."

Sir Bedivere, greatly grieving, took Excalibur from its sheath and went to the water's edge. But the sword was so wonderful that he could not throw it away, so he hid it and returned to Arthur.

"What did you see?" Arthur asked.

"Only the waters and the waves," replied Bedivere.

"You have tried to trick me," sighed Arthur. "Go now and throw it into the waters if you love me."

But again Bedivere could not bring himself to part with the beautiful sword.

The third time, however, Bedivere followed his king's commands and threw the sword as far into the lake as he could. Then he beheld a wondrous sight. A hand came up from the water, caught the sword, and vanished under the water.

Bedivere returned to Arthur with this message.

"That is good," replied Arthur. "Now take me down to the shore of the lake."

There by the shore was a barge with three

queens clothed in black and a number of weeping women. Arthur was laid in the barge by his fairy sister Morgana, the Lady of the Lake, the Fairy Queen of North Wales, and their fairy maidens.

"Fear not," the king called to Bedivere, "for I go to the Isle of Avalon to be cured of my wounds."

And so King Arthur disappeared into the distance.

But it is said that he will come again at a time when England is in sore need of a great ruler.

Others say that his body was found and buried, and on the tombstone appeared the words, "Here Arthur lies, King that Was and King that Shall Be."

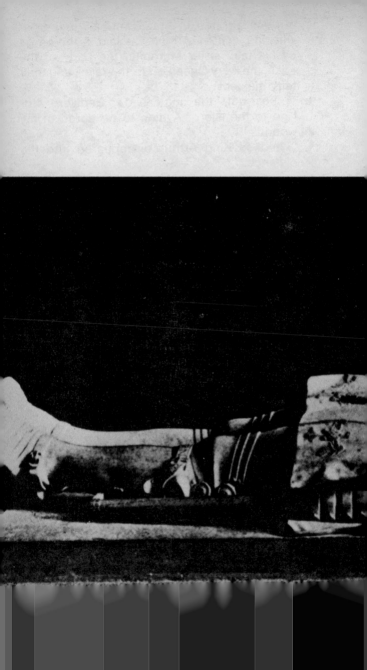

The highest type of ruler is one of whose existence
the people are barely aware.
Next comes one whom they love and praise.
Next comes one whom they fear.
Next comes one whom they despise and defy.

The sage is self-effacing and scanty of words.
When his task is accomplished and things have been
completed
All the people say, "We ourselves have achieved it!"
TAO TE CHING

GODS AND KINGS

A very important function of mythology was to give supernatural or at least historical legitimacy to government. Almost every tribe has some sort of legend about the beginning of its government or the founding of its dynasty. The myth may invest the king with divine blessing by some kind of sign, as when Arthur pulled the sword out of the stone. Or the ruling family may actually be considered to be the descendants of their god.

JAPANESE

Amaterasu, the Japan sun goddess, decided to send her son over the rainbow bridge to earth to rule Japan. But the world below was full of disturbances and he refused to go. Three other gods were sent to the land below before the disturbances were quelled.

Ame-no-Wakahiko, one of the bravest of the gods, finally went to the earth and married the daughter of a prominent sorcerer. For eight years he stayed in the land below and the gods in heaven heard nothing from him.

At last they sent a pheasant to find out what had happened to him. One of the women in the palace came running to Ame-no-Wakahiko to tell him that a bird of ill-omen had appeared at the palace, and the god rushed out and shot the pheasant from heaven. The arrow pierced the messenger of the gods and went all the way up to heaven, where the gods cursed it and sent it back. The arrow struck Ame-no-Wakahiko and killed him. The god's parents went to earth for the great funeral.

Then Amaterasu, the sun goddess, sent her grandson, Ninigi, to earth to rule over it. As presents she gave him the sword Kusanagi which had been found in the tail of an eight-headed snake, heavenly jewels, and a sacred mirror. These three objects became the emblems of imperial power, and Ninigi became the father of the imperial family of Japan.

INCAN

The men who lived upon earth lived in ignorance and fear. They had no llamas, did not know how to grow crops, and did not know how to build houses. But Inti, the sun, took pity upon them and sent his son and daughter to mankind. He set them in a boat on Lake Titicaca and gave them his golden staff.

When the children of the sun found men, they taught them how to live together peacefully. They taught them to marry and live in families and how to choose leaders. They showed the men how to grow corn and tame llamas and make clothes from their wool. Gold, silver, and clay were also their gifts, and they showed them how to build houses and temples. They also taught the rules that were given unto the Incas.

Before they left, they told the people that the sun himself had adopted the Incas as his children and chosen them to rule over the rest of the world. And from that time on the Incas ruled the land and spread the worship of the sun among all the tribes of the land.

EGYPTIAN

In Egypt, all of the rulers traced their ancestry to Osiris, the first king who on his death became the god of the dead. After their deaths, the pharaohs were also referred to as Osiris.

As the first pharaoh, Osiris found a very primitive people. He abolished cannibalism and taught them farming and how to build cities and temples. All the glories of Egypt began with the reign of Osiris.

legal riddles

In Africa, many tribes were ruled by a democratic council of all the men of the village. Reaching agreement among 10,000 men was sometimes difficult, so many tribes spent much time practicing their skills in judgment on riddles and famous cases of the past. The most difficult riddles were handed down from generation to generation and solutions were debated for years.

There were once three youths who loved a beautiful maiden. She could not choose between them so she told them all to go off and prove themselves men.

Each of the young men had a magic gift from his ancestors. The first had a magic mirror which would let him see anything in the world. So while the men were away from their sweetheart, they looked in the mirror every night to see their beloved. But one night as they saw her, she was stretched on the ground dead and everyone around was mourning.

So the second young man took his magic gift, a fan which would take him anywhere he wanted to go. He waved the fan and the three young men were instantly back in their home.

The third young man then took out his gift—a cow-tailed switch which would bring a person back to life. He waved it over the girl and she came back to life.

The question is: Which of the men should she marry?

There was once a wealthy man who died. No one came to mourn at his funeral except a sparrow and a parrot.

280

So when it was time to divide his wealth, the chief and councillors asked these two birds what claim they had to the wealth.

"I was the man's best friend," replied the sparrow. "I followed him wherever he went and cheered him with my song. He fed me and enjoyed my company. I have only the claim of friendship."

"I am the cause of his wealth," said the parrot. "For the man started his trading with a robe made from my feathers. The man took me from my home in the forest so he could become wealthy. It is only right that I should inherit his wealth."

Whose claim is most valid?

the phoenix

There was once a small sparrow who laid three eggs in her nest, but a mouse came and ate two of them.

Heartbroken, she rushed off to the queen of birds, the phoenix, to beg for justice.

"I have no time to listen to you," replied the phoenix. "You are just a small, ugly bird. It is the job of parents to look after their own children. Don't bother me with your complaint."

So the sparrow returned home, determined to take things into her own hands. The next day she pretended to leave her nest and saw the mouse coming to eat the remaining egg. But this time she rushed down and pecked his eye out. Crazed by the pain and blind, he rushed into the nostril of a lion who was sleeping by the shore of a lake.

282

and the sparrow

A dragon was resting in the lake, and he was so startled by the lion that he jumped right out of the water, knocking the phoenix's nest with her one egg into the water.

The phoenix screamed in rage and flew to punish the dragon. But the dragon blamed the lion who had frightened him. The lion claimed that it was the mouse's fault, and the mouse blamed the sparrow.

But when the phoenix went to the sparrow, seeking justice for her loss, the sparrow only replied, "Queen, you told me that it is the duty of parents to look after their children, that the state could not be bothered with such trifles. I think you have nothing to blame but your own carelessness."

the tragedies of thebes

"Your child is cursed," Tiresias warned Laius, "for he shall kill his father and marry his mother."

What could Laius do? He could not bring himself to kill his son so he sent a slave to expose the child on a mountain. To make certain the child did not escape, his feet were pierced and tied together with a thong.

But a kindly shepherd found the child and took him to Polybus, the king of Corinth, who

adopted him, and called him Oedipus, or Swollen Feet. When he grew up, Oedipus wanted to find out who his real parents were, so he went to ask the oracle of Apollo. But instead of answering, the oracle repeated the horrible prophecy: "You will kill your father and marry your mother."

Knowing no parents but Polybus, Oedipus fled from Corinth. But man cannot escape his fate. For on the road, Oedipus met an old man, quarreled with him, and killed him. The old man was none other than his father, Laius, who was also traveling to Delphi to ask how the Sphinx might be killed.

Knowing none of this, Oedipus continued on his journey and soon met the Sphinx. The Sphinx was a strange creature, half woman, half lion, who challenged everyone she met with a riddle, "What goes on four feet when a child, two feet when in the middle of life, and three feet when old?"

"A man," replied Oedipus, thus breaking the Sphinx's power and freeing the city of Thebes from her curse. The grateful city made Oedipus their king, and Jocasta, the widow of the dead king, married him.

For several years they lived happily and had four children. But eventually a plague came upon the city. Again the oracle was consulted and the message was:

"The murder of Laius has never been avenged."

Not knowing that he himself was the murderer, Oedipus sent for all of the wise men of the country.

"Do not ask for the answer," the old prophet Tiresias warned, "for you may discover more than you want to know."

But Oedipus did not heed his warning. Grad-

285

ually the story was unraveled. The prophecy that Laius would be killed by his own son was recalled, and Oedipus trembled as he remembered the prophecy made about himself. The old slave who had exposed the child on the mountain was sent for, and Oedipus shuddered as he described the child's pierced feet.

A man who had witnessed the death of Laius did not recognize Oedipus but described the crossroads accurately, and Oedipus could remember the old man he killed. At last no doubt was possible, for the shepherd who took Oedipus to King Polybus was found and told his part of the story.

Jocasta, too, had been listening to the story in horror and, even before Oedipus, realized the horrible fact—she was married to her own son! She ran from the room and hanged herself. Oedipus followed her and after he saw her dead body, he tore his eyes out of their sockets in penance for the crime he had unknowingly committed.

Led by his faithful daughter, Antigone, Oedipus wandered from land to land, until at last he was sent to Colonus by Apollo, where he was purged of his sins and died in peace. His bones were revered as a holy spot which would protect the country from invaders.

But the troubles of the family were not over. Oedipus' two sons, Eteocles and Polynices, quarreled over the kingdom. Eteocles, the eldest, became the king, and Polynices and six powerful allies attacked the city in a battle which has become known as Seven Against Thebes. Both brothers were killed.

Creon, Oedipus' uncle, assumed control of the city and decreed that the rebellious brother, Polynices, would not be allowed proper burial rites, and his body was to be left for the dogs.

This was a horrible punishment, for the Greeks believed that a person who was not buried properly could not go to the land of the dead. It was also a terrible conflict for Antigone, Polynices' sister. On the one hand, the legal ruler of the city had decreed that Polynices should not be buried. The force and power of the law was on his side. But on the other side was the higher law of the gods which placed family loyalty among the most important virtues. To complicate the conflict, Antigone was in love with Haemon, Creon's son, and was planning to marry him.

But Antigone was the girl who had gone with her disgraced father into exile. So now she chose to disobey the law of the land rather than her obligation to her dead brother. In the night, she slipped by the drowsy guards and sprinkled dirt over her brother's body.

Enraged at this defiance of his authority, Creon ordered his men to find the culprit and ordered him to be put to death. He was dismayed when his men brought Antigone before him and she admitted the crime.

But Creon felt that he could not allow even someone from his own family to disregard his authority and he refused to listen to Antigone's claims that his law was unjust. He sentenced her to be buried alive in her family tomb.

His son Haemon pleaded for mercy, but Creon became more adamant in his anger that his own son would dare to defy him.

Finally Tiresias, the old blind prophet, appeared. "You must not defy the gods by making a law contrary to their teachings," he urged.

But Creon defied even this revered figure. "I'm not going to listen to you, for you have probably been bribed by Antigone's friends," he replied.

Tiresias left in anger. "You will pay for this arrogance by the time the sun goes down today," he warned.

At last Creon began to relent and sent a messenger to release Antigone from the tomb. But the messenger returned sorrowfully. Antigone was already dead. She had hanged herself. And worse than that, Haemon, Creon's son, had hanged himself by her side. A horrible cry went up at this news, and before Creon could return home, word came that his wife had committed suicide when she heard of her son's death.

Creon did not die. He lived and ruled for many more lonely years. But from then on he was a good ruler and never again made laws that went against the commands of the gods.

the trojan war

One day in a feast on Mount Olympus, a beautiful golden apple appeared with this inscription, "This apple belongs to the most beautiful goddess." Immediately, of course, there was an uproar for the apple. Athena, Hera, and Aphrodite angrily went to Zeus demanding that he decide between them, but he wisely refused: "Find some mortal to judge," he suggested. So the three goddesses decided to submit the case to Paris, son of Priam, the king of Troy.

But none of the goddesses was willing to trust to her beauty alone. Athena attempted to bribe Paris by offering to lead him to victory over the Greeks. Hera offered to make him lord of Europe and Asia, and Aphrodite offered him the most beautiful woman in the world.

Paris' choice was for Aphrodite and the most beautiful woman in the world. How poor a choice that was was revealed by later events. For the most beautiful woman in the world was Helen, who was already married to Menelaus, one of the most powerful of the Greeks. Furthermore, all of the Greek chieftains had sworn an oath that if anyone tried to kidnap Helen, they would go to Menelaus' defense.

Paris disregarded all of this, however, and set out with Aphrodite for Helen's home. Menelaus received him warmly, not suspecting the treachery he planned, and he trusted him so much that he went on a trip to Crete, leaving his wife with Paris. Paris, of course, set off for Troy with Helen as soon as her husband was gone.

Menelaus returned to find Helen gone and immediately called for all of the chieftains of

Greece to help him get his wife back and also to burn Troy to the ground. The Greeks, who still regarded piracy as a fairly honorable occupation, were eager to go for the glory of war and the chance of obtaining the spoils of the wealthy Troy.

However, even in that day there were some who opposed war, and their tactics hardly differed from those of modern draft resisters. Odysseus did not want to leave his wife and young son, so he pretended to be mad. When the messengers of Menelaus arrived, they found him plowing the seashore and sowing it with salt. But the messengers put his young son in front of the plow, and when Odysseus stopped, they knew he was not mad.

Achilles was more than willing to go to war, but his mother refused to allow him. She dressed him as a woman and attempted to conceal him in that way. Ironically, Odysseus was sent to get Achilles, and he disguised himself as a peddler, taking into the women's quarters a load of silks and jewelry and also a load of armor. Only one "young lady" showed interest in the armor, and Odysseus knew that he had found Achilles.

The Greek army was finally gathered at Aulis to sail, but the winds were so strong that they could not go. At last a prophet claimed that they had offended Artemis and could only regain her favor by sacrificing Iphigenia, the daughter of Agamemnon. So eager for battle was Agamemnon that he did not hesitate to make this sacrifice and sent for his daughter immediately.

After the death of Iphigenia, the Greeks sailed for Troy. But the battle was not destined to be a quick one. The gods themselves took sides, with Aphrodite, of course, helping the

Trojans, and Hera and Athena on the side of the Greeks. Ares, who was in love with Aphrodite, sided with her, and Apollo and his sister Artemis also favored the Trojans. Zeus himself leaned toward the Trojans, but tried to remain neutral. Poseidon, however, favored the Greeks, for they were a seafaring people and were diligent in the sacrifices to him.

Troy had great human champions, too, particularly Hector, the son of King Priam. The battle raged for nine years with neither side being very successful. Then a quarrel arose among the Greeks.

The Greeks had captured two women and had given them to their two greatest warriors, Agamemnon, their leader, and Achilles. But the girl who had been given to Agamemnon was the daughter of a priest of Apollo, and Apollo sent a plague among the Greeks.

Thousands of Greeks were dying from sickness when finally a soothsayer told them that the plague was sent because of Apollo's priest's daughter. Agamemnon did not take this news very well and said that if his woman were taken away from him, that he must have Achilles' girl.

Achilles took his loss with even worse grace and decided to have nothing to do with the war until he got his girl back. So he sat in his tent with his friend Patroclus and pouted while all of the other warriors went out to battle.

In contrast to the squabbles among the Greeks, the Trojan camp seemed calm and peaceful. Hector spent his time with his beloved wife, Andromache, and his young son, Astyanax. Helen walked among the troops, building up their morale, for they had only to look at her to feel that the battle was worth fighting.

In the midst of the battle, a sensible solution

seemed to have emerged. Paris and Menelaus became engaged in combat, and the troops pulled back to watch, apparently agreeing to let these two fight it out themselves. But Aphrodite was not willing to let it be a fair fight, for she knew that her hero, Paris, was the weaker. So she broke Menelaus' sword. Undaunted, he grabbed Paris by the helmet and began to drag him back to the Greeks in victory. But Aphrodite broke the helmet strap and took Paris up in a cloud of dust.

The gods continued to interfere in the war, trying to protect their special champions. Aeneas, one of the heroes of Troy, was Aphrodite's own son and she tried to protect him from Diomedes, one of the Trojan leaders. But Diomedes was not afraid of the gods and he dealt Aphrodite a blow on the hand which sent her crying back to Mount Olympus. Even braver, Diomedes wounded Ares, the god of war himself, with his spear. Ares turned out not to be a very good warrior after all, and he, too, went crying back to Olympus. Zeus laughed at both of them.

Even with their two immortal helpers gone, the Trojans seemed to be winning the battle, for the loss of Achilles for the Greeks seemed to be worse than the loss of both Ares and Aphrodite for the Trojans. At last the Greeks realized that they would have to try to appease Achilles or the battle would be lost. But there seemed to be no way to win back Achilles. In fact, when Odysseus and Nestor came bringing back his woman and lots of other gifts, he said that he was sailing for home and they need not trouble themselves any more.

The next day the battle became even worse for the Greeks. The Trojans were close enough to success that it seemed that they would soon be able to set the Greeks' ships on fire and therefore be able to kill them all. Patroclus said that he would no longer stay out of the war on his friend's account and asked if he could borrow Achilles' armor.

"All right," Achilles agreed. "Take my armor and my men, too. I will not fight until they get to my own ships."

Of

So Patroclus went to battle in Achilles' famous armor. The Trojans were upset at seeing Achilles again and began to retreat, until Hector himself came to fight in single combat. Patroclus fought bravely, but he was no match for Hector and was soon killed. Hector stripped off Achilles' armor and put it on himself.

Achilles was almost crazed with grief when he heard of the death of his friend. "I cannot live if my friend is dead," he cried, and those around him feared that he would commit suicide. But his mother, Thetis, who was a goddess, appeared and tried to calm him. Soon his cries changed to warnings of revenge on Hector.

"Achilles," Thetis reminded him sadly. "Remember that you are fated to die soon after Hector dies."

"What do I care about that!" he shouted. "If Hector is dead, I will be glad to join my friend Patroclus in Hades."

Seeing that he was determined to fight Hector, Thetis hurried to Olympus where she asked Hephaestus himself to make him armor.

Everyone knew from prophecies that Hector was doomed to die at Achilles' hand, but Hector still fought bravely. The rest of the men, sensing their doom, fled behind the walls of Troy. Priam and Hecuba, his parents, begged Hector to come in, too, but he refused.

However, when Hector saw Achilles coming after him with Athena by his side, he turned and fled. Three times around the walls of Troy they raced before Hector finally turned and faced his pursuers. It was an uneven fight from the start. Athena turned Hector's spear away from Achilles, but guided Achilles' aim. Apollo knew that it was hopeless to try to help his hero and so left him to his death.

Achilles aimed his spear at a weak spot in what had so recently been his own armor, and great Hector fell.

"Please return my body to my parents," Hector breathed as he fell, but Achilles even took vengeance on the dead body. "I would like to eat your raw flesh!" Achilles cried. "I certainly will not let you have a proper burial." He fastened the body to his chariot and dragged it round and round the walls of Troy.

But Zeus refused to allow this disregard of the laws of the gods. He sent a messenger to Priam telling him to take gifts to Achilles and beg for the body. When the old man appeared before Achilles and humbly clasped his knees, the great hero felt a strange pity and treated his enemy kindly. He offered to stop the battle for as long as was needed for the funeral rites.

Nine days the Trojans mourned for Hector, and even the Greeks watched respectfully the funeral of the great hero they could not help admiring. For Hector was not only the bravest and strongest of Troy's heroes, he was also a gentle husband and father and an obedient son and a kind ruler whom everyone had loved.

With Hector gone, the end of the battle was

in sight, for all knew that Achilles was fated to die soon after Hector. He was finally killed by an arrow which Paris shot from the walls of Troy.

Ajax, another great hero, died soon after. The Greeks voted to decide who should receive Achilles' armor, which had been made by Hephaestus. Ajax and Odysseus were the two contenders, and when Odysseus won, Ajax went mad. He went through the Greek camp killing sheep and cattle, thinking they were Trojans. When he came to himself, he was so humiliated that he killed himself.

The Greeks were disheartened by the deaths of two of their greatest heroes. A soothsayer told them that they could never take Troy until they had the bow and arrow of Hercules.

When they heard this oracle, the Greeks realized that they were being punished for another crime they had committed on the way to Troy. Philoctetes, who owned Hercules' bow and arrow, had been bitten by a scorpion, and when the wound would not heal, the Greeks had abandoned him on an uninhabited island.

GrEEks

So Odysseus and Diomedes were sent to find the bow, and Philoctetes, if they could. They found Philoctetes alive and brought him on to Troy where a physician managed to cure his foot. As soon as he was well, he went into battle. His first victim was Paris.

But still the battle continued, and the Greeks saw no hope of conquering the city. At last Odysseus thought of a plan. He had a skilled craftsman build a huge wooden horse. Then one night, they wheeled the horse up to the gates of Troy, and the best of the Greek soldiers hid themselves inside it. The other Greeks withdrew to their ships.

The next morning, the Trojans were joyful to see the Greeks gone. But they were still suspicious. The Greeks had a further plan though. The Trojans found one man left in the Greek camp. He greeted the Trojans gladly, saying that the Greeks had given up the fight and were sailing home. The gods had demanded a human sacrifice and he had been the man chosen. He had escaped and now wanted to join the Trojans.

The Trojans welcomed him and took him through the Greek camp. When they came upon the great horse, he told them that the Greeks had made it as a sacrifice to Athena whom they had offended. They hoped that the Trojans would burn it and therefore bring down her wrath upon them. They especially hoped that the Trojans would not bring it into the city, as it would bring them good fortune.

Only four of the Trojans doubted the story. Laocoön and his two sons warned, "Beware of Greeks bringing gifts." Cassandra, the prophetess, also warned them. But Poseidon sent a sea monster who killed Laocoön and his two sons before the very eyes of the Greek army, and nobody ever believed Cassandra, so the Trojans hurriedly took the horse inside, fearing that Poseidon would kill more of them.

That night the Greeks crept out of the horse and opened the gates. The Greek ships had returned and all of the troops slipped inside. The Greeks had already begun setting fire to the town by the time the Trojans woke up.

The slaughter was complete. Of all of the warriors, only Aeneas, who was protected by Aphrodite, escaped. Helen was returned to

Menelaus, but the fate of the other Trojan women was much harder.

The Trojan War, through Homer's great poem, the *Iliad,* has become the symbol of the glories of war. But a later writer, Euripides, used it to show the horrors of war, in his play *The Trojan Women* which showed the suffering of Andromache and Hecuba and the other women of Troy as the Greeks captured them and led them away into slavery.

BeARINg

giffs

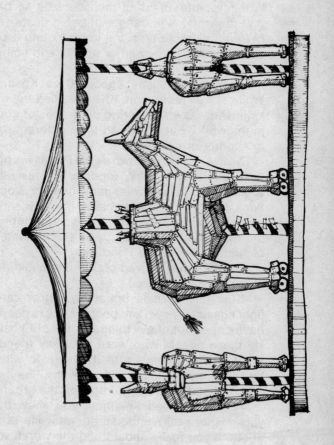

arjuna's duty

Whenever the affairs of men become so bad that the world is in danger of being destroyed before the proper time, the great Vishnu takes on the form of a human or animal and comes to earth.

So it was when he appeared as Krishna. While still a young man, Krishna killed the evil king who was endangering the forces of good in the world. But he stayed for a different role in another great battle.

The five brothers known as the Pandavas had been deprived of their kingdom by their relatives, the Kurus, and after many other provocations, finally went to war against them. Krishna, who was kin to both groups, did not fight in the war but agreed to serve as the charioteer of Arjuna, one of the Pandavas.

But when they arrived on the battlefield, Arjuna suddenly stopped.

"Krishna," he said unhappily, "how can I fight against my own kinspeople? These people have done a lot of evil things to me, but I can't kill these people who were once my friends. What is a kingdom worth if I have to win it by killing my friends? I will not fight," he said and dropped his powerful bow on the ground.

"Arjuna," replied Krishna, "you show that you do not really understand what life is all about. If you really understood the world, you would know that this life is only a brief part of the many lives you will go through. There is no way that you can kill someone or be killed. For the spirit was never born and will never end. Each life on this earth is like taking off

one pair of clothes and putting on another. But the life itself goes on.

"Birth leads to death and death leads to birth. So why are you upset? In this birth you were born a Kshattria, a warrior, and your task is to engage in war. If you do not kill those ordained to die, they will suffer unnecessarily in this life and you will not return as you should.

"So, Arjuna, you must go into the battle and fight, knowing that you are doing the right thing even if you must kill your friends and kinsmen."

For days Krishna taught Arjuna the secrets of life and death, and at last Arjuna was ready to go into battle. There he succeeded in killing his enemies, but he did not gloat over their slaughter. For he now knew that he was only doing the duty for which he had been born in this life.

the five nations

Many years ago there was a chief of the Onondagas who was unhappy at the way his people were always fighting. Even the Oneidas and the Senecas, who were their close relatives, were always fighting them. One day he called his two sons to him and said, "I have had a vision. The Great Spirit has shown me that you, my two sons, are to bring peace to our people. So go from me now on a quest for peace and do not return until you have established it."

The two young men were very troubled, for they had no idea how to fulfill their father's request. They traveled until they came to a river with high rocks jutting over it.

"The quest our father has given us is beyond the possibility of human beings," said the oldest brother. "There is no way for us to fulfill it, but a son who cannot obey his father does not deserve to live. I see nothing for us to do but climb those rocks and cast ourselves off into the river."

So, sorrowfully, the two boys began to climb the rocks and walk toward the cliff. But as they reached the edge, they saw a strange canoe coming across the river and in it was an old man with white hair. He saw the two brothers and beckoned to them to come down from the rocks.

"Why are you trying to end your lives?" the stranger asked.

"Our father has given us a task which we cannot do," said the brothers. "And a son who cannot obey his father does not deserve to live."

"You have given up too quickly," replied the

303

old man. "For I can show you the way to obey his command. Go and gather firewood."

The brothers stood staring at the old man in amazement at this strange command.

But suddenly his eyes flashed like lightning. "When you are lost and someone tells you how to go, do you refuse to follow them?"

The boys immediately began to gather firewood and made a great pile.

"Build a fire," said the strange old man, and this time the boys did not hesitate. After they finished, they looked up expectantly, but the old man was preparing to leave.

"Now," he said, "all the tribes around will see your council fire and will come to you. You must keep the fire going until your father's command has been obeyed and peace has come."

"But what shall we do when the people come?" asked the boys.

"I will return when you need me," replied the old man as he stepped in his canoe and started off.

So the brothers waited until the Mohawks, the Onondagas, the Senecas, the Oneidas, and the Cayugas all came together. Each tribe came suspiciously and brought weapons. All day and night the brothers waited for the old man to return. But he did not come. Instead, something else happened. A strange power seemed to come over the two brothers, and at last the eldest brother rose to speak.

"Brothers," he said, "I have called you together because the Great Spirit has spoken to me. Let there be no more war among us, but let us smoke the pipe of peace. As long as we quarrel among ourselves, we cannot become a great nation." As he spoke, it seemed as if a golden light were around his head. And when he finished, he hurled his battle ax into the fire, and all of the other chiefs followed his example.

Then he took from his belt the peace pipe and the chiefs made a treaty among themselves and formed the League of the Iroquois. The pipe passed from one chief to another until it finally came to a strange old man, whom the brothers immediately recognized as their teacher.

"You have done well," he said to the two brothers, "for you have followed the commands of the Great Spirit. From now on, your people will be a great nation. My task is completed and now I must go."

"Before you go, please tell us your name," said the brothers.

"I am known by many names," he replied, "but you may call me Hiawatha."

MANKIND'S DREAM OF PEACE

Most mythologies glorify the leader who united their own tribe and brought peace to their land, and many go beyond this parochial peace to prophesy that someday in the future there will come a leader who will unite all of mankind and will bring peace forever to earth.

N O R S E

From the wrecks of the old world and the destruction of the old gods, a new world will be born. The earth itself will rise again from the waves of the ocean. Mountains will rise anew. Corn will again grow in the valleys. The eagle will fly in the sky and the sun again will shine.

Then Balder, the fairest of the old gods, the first of the gods to die, will be reborn, and with him his loving brother Hoder.

And then from the center of the great ash tree Yggdrasil, the few people who have survived the great conflagration will return.

krig är inte sunt för barn och andra levande ting

Swedish

306

HEBREW

And there shall come forth a rod out of the stem of Jesse, and a Branch shall grow out of his roots.

And the spirit of the Lord shall rest upon him, and the spirit of wisdom and understanding, the spirit of counsel and might, the spirit of knowledge and of the fear of the Lord . . .

The wolf also shall dwell with the lamb, and the leopard shall lie down with the kid; and the calf and the young lion and the fatling together; and a little child shall lead them . . .

They shall not hurt nor destroy in all my holy mountain; for the earth shall be full of the knowledge of the Lord, as the waters cover the sea.

ISAIAH 11:1-2, 6, 9

Hebrew

Vietnamese

Spanish

Russian

Chinese

Hindu

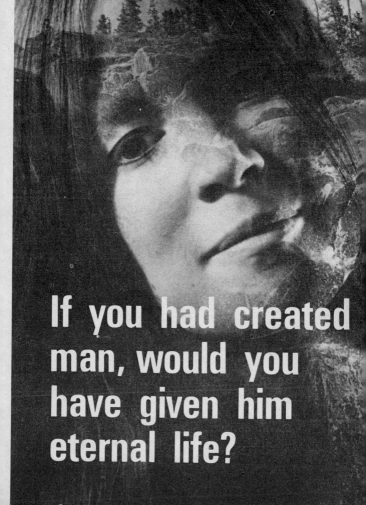

If you had created man, would you have given him eternal life?

IS DEATH THE END?

the dilemma of old man and old woman

Old Man and Old Woman reached a very difficult problem in planning the destiny of man. They had decided what man would look like and what kind of work he would do. Now they had to decide about death.

"Should man die for four days and then come back to life, or should he die and remain dead?" asked Old Woman.

Old Man said, "I know how to decide. I will throw a buffalo chip into the water. If it floats, man will die for four days and then come back to life. If it sinks, man will die forever."

Old Man threw the buffalo chip into the water and it sank. Man was to die forever.

Some time later Old Man and Old Woman had a daughter. While she was still young, she died. Old Woman said, "I have changed my mind about death. I now think that man should die for four days and then come back to life. I want my daughter back."

"It is too late," said Old Man. "We have already decided. Let us not change our minds."

312

gilgamesh

BABYLONIAN

Enkidu was dead. And Gilgamesh, the mightiest hero of the ancient world, was helpless. Gilgamesh, who had conquered fierce monsters, who wrestled with lions barehanded, who had dared refuse the wooing of the jealous goddess Ishtar, could do nothing to save his friend from death.

For days Gilgamesh wept beside the body of his friend, refusing to bury him, but at last he realized that there was nothing more he could do for Enkidu. But with the prospect of death before him, Gilgamesh could not return happily to his old life of killing enemies and monsters. The only monster he now wanted to fight was death.

At last Gilgamesh heard of Utnapishtim, the only mortal who had ever escaped death, and resolved to visit him. But Utnapishtim lived beyond the rim of the world, on the mountain of Mashu, where no man had ever been before.

The first obstacle was the scorpion-men who guarded the entrance to the mountains at the rim of the world. The chief of the scorpion-men tried to convince Gilgamesh that his journey was futile, but Gilgamesh could not be dissuaded and was allowed to continue. Next he met a barmaid in an ale house. Horrified at his goal, she too told him the journey was futile.

"The gods have decreed that mankind must die," she said. "The best thing for you to do is to enjoy the life that you have instead of wasting it looking for immortality."

But when Gilgamesh refused to listen to her, she pointed the way to the Sea of Death and the boatman, Urshanabi, who could take him across.

> 66 Whoever has lived long enough to find out what life is knows how deep a debt of gratitude we owe to Adam, the first great benefactor of our race. He brought death into the world. 99
>
> MARK TWAIN

Urshanabi, too, tried to dissuade Gilgamesh, but finally agreed to ferry him across the river if he could cut 120 poles to use in the journey. "For," he said, "no pole can touch the Waters of Death more than once."

Upon his arrival, Utnapishtim and his wife welcomed Gilgamesh to their home and treated him kindly. But Utnapishtim only shook his head when he heard Gilgamesh's request. "Since the beginning of time," he said, "everything has come to an end."

Gilgamesh was not satisfied: "If that is true, how do you have eternal life?"

> 66 If I pass this test do I get immortal life as a prize? Think what a bummer that would be. Fear of death puts a little excitement into life. 99
>
> Anonymous respondent to PSYCHOLOGY TODAY questionnaire on death

"It was a gift from the gods," Utnapishtim replied. "Long ago I lived by the Euphrates. The gods became angry at the rapid growth of men who were disturbing their peace, so they decided to send a great flood to destroy everyone. However, Ea, the water god, warned me of the danger and told me to build a large ship and take with me the seeds of every living thing. For seven days the waters poured down on the earth and the earth was completely covered with water. All mankind except my wife and I turned back into clay. When the rains stopped, I sent out a dove and a swallow to look for dry land, but they could not find any and returned. Some time later I sent out a raven who searched and found food and a resting place. Then I knew that the flood was over, and released all of the animals and gave thanks to the gods. It was then that I was given immortality. But I was removed from the world of men, for the gift was not to be shared with the rest."

Gilgamesh, however, continued to plead for immortality. Finally Utnapishtim began to lose his patience. "You wouldn't know what to do with immortality if you had it! Why do you want to live forever, when you cannot even stay awake more than sixteen hours at a time?"

"I can too," replied Gilgamesh.

"I will make you a bet," said Utnapishtim.

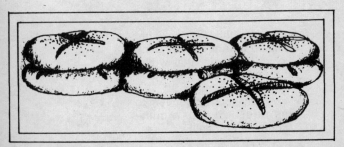

"I'll bet that you cannot stay awake for seven days and seven nights."

The first two days Gilgamesh stayed awake with no trouble. But by the third day the struggle was becoming more difficult. By the fifth day, he was wrestling with sleep harder than he had ever wrestled with lions. By the sixth day he was asleep.

For each day he slept, Utnapishtim's wife baked a cake. When Gilgamesh awoke seven days later, instead of immortality he only had seven cakes to show that he could not even stay awake. Thus Gilgamesh lost his chance for eternal life.

Death is the price we pay for give ground to the bright and new.
meaningful life. Death makes way. Death wipes clean and prepares
Death forces the tired and old to the ground for new advance.
ISAAC ASIMOV

318

the moon or the banana

One day God asked the first human couple, who then lived in heaven, what kind of death they wanted—that of the moon or that of the banana. The couple wondered what the difference was, so God explained: The banana puts forth shoots that take its place and the moon itself comes back to life.

The couple considered for a long time before they made their choice. If they decided to be childless, they could avoid death for themselves, but they would also be very lonely and would themselves have to carry out all of the work and would not have anyone to work and strive for.

So they asked God for children, well aware of the consequences of their choice. And their request was granted.

Since that time man's time on this earth is very short.

the cow-tailed switch

One morning Ogaloussa went out to hunt, leaving behind his wife and sons. But that night he did not come home. No one knew what had happened to him.

A few months later another son named Puli was born to Ogaloussa's wife. As soon as he could talk, he asked, "Where is my father?"

"We do not know," replied his brothers.

"Why don't you find out?" asked Puli.

The older brothers set out into the forest following their father's trail. At last they came to a clearing where they found Ogaloussa's bones and his rusted weapons.

The oldest son stepped forward. "I know how to put a dead person's bones together." So with the help of the others, he reassembled the skeleton.

The second son said, "I know how to put flesh and sinews on the bones," and so he did.

The third son then stepped forward and put breath into the body.

Ogaloussa opened his eyes and looked around him, picked up his weapons, and went home with his sons.

Then he took his most prized possession—a cow-tail switch. "This," he said, "is my finest possession. I want to show my gratitude to my sons, but I have only one switch to give, so I will give it to the son who did the most to bring me back to life."

With that, he stepped up to Puli and put the switch in his hand.

And the people knew that he had made the right choice, for it is said that a man is not really dead until he is forgotten.

320

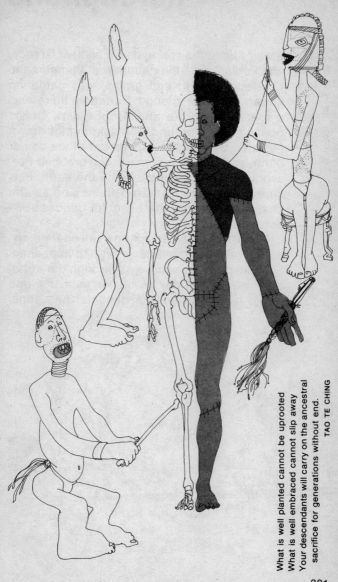

What is well planted cannot be uprooted
What is well embraced cannot slip away
Your descendants will carry on the ancestral
sacrifice for generations without end.

TAO TE CHING

321

persephone

It was a beautiful spring day in ancient Greece, and Persephone, the daughter of Demeter, the goddess of earth and grains, was gathering flowers with her friends. Suddenly there was a great earthquake and a huge dark chasm opened in the ground. A black chariot drawn by fiery black horses dashed out of the center of the earth and a fearsome man grabbed Persephone and rushed back into the earth. Persephone's friends stared in horror as the chasm closed and the beautiful goddess disappeared.

Demeter heard Persephone's desperate cry, but no one dared tell her what had happened. For nine days she wandered through the world, but neither bird nor plant nor man nor god would tell her where her daughter had gone.

322

At last, she forced Helius, the god of the sun, who sees everything, to tell her the truth. But the truth did not bring Demeter relief from her sorrows. Persephone had been kidnapped by Hades, the god of the dead.

Furious, Demeter demanded that Zeus force Hades to release her daughter. But Hades was Zeus' brother, and a powerful god who was not to be trifled with. Besides, Hades really loved Persephone and had resorted to kidnapping her only after Zeus had refused his proper petition to marry her.

But Demeter was not one to trifle with either. In anger and sorrow she wandered through the earth. She spent some time with a friendly family, serving as a nurse to one of the children. Knowing the sorrow of the death of a child, she tried to make the boy immortal by laying him in the fire. One night the mother woke up and screamed when she saw the flames about her son. Then Demeter revealed herself to them, and the grateful family built her a temple.

There she stayed in sorrow, and all of the earth sorrowed with her. Slowly the leaves on the trees turned brown and fell off. Slowly the grain in the fields dried and withered. No new seeds sprouted and all vegetation died. It was as if the earth itself were dying in sorrow for the loss of Persephone.

Zeus realized that Demeter had won, and reluctantly he sent Hermes to tell Hades that he must release Persephone. Hades was angry, but Persephone had refused to eat or to come near him all of the time she had been there, so he reluctantly agreed to let her go. "However," he said, "if she had eaten anything I could not let her go, because no one can return to the land of the living after eating the food of the dead."

At this, Ascalaphus, Hades' gardener, jumped up and cried, "Then she can't go back, for I saw her eat some pomegranate seeds!" Demeter angrily turned Ascalaphus into an owl. But it was too late. He was right. Persephone had eaten the food of the dead.

The problem was too complicated even for Zeus to solve, so he called on his mother, Rhea, to help. Rhea compromised by deciding that Persephone would spend half of the year above the ground with her mother and half of the year in the land of the dead with her husband, Hades.

Hades seems to have accepted the compromise well, but Demeter still sorrows every year when her beloved daughter must return to the land of the dead. And every year, as Persephone leaves, Demeter and all of the earth sorrow. Leaves turn brown and fall to the ground, and grain and vegetables wither and die.

But each spring, Persephone returns to life and brings with her flowers and all of the plants that men and animals depend on for life.

Except a corn of wheat fall into the ground and die, it abideth alone: but if it die, it bringeth forth much fruit.

JOHN 12:24

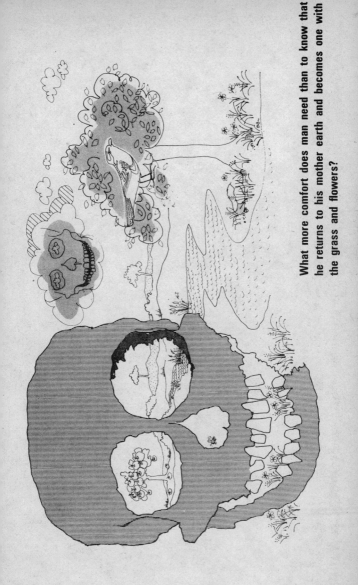

What more comfort does man need than to know that he returns to his mother earth and becomes one with the grass and flowers?

osiris

EGYPTIAN

Son of the earth god and the sky goddess, Osiris was the mythological first king of Egypt. Ruling with his sister and wife, Isis, he brought to the Egyptians the gifts of agriculture. When he began to rule, the Egyptians were savage cannibals, but Isis discovered barley and wheat and taught the people to grow them, and Osiris discovered fruit trees and grapevines. His people were so pleased by these gifts that Osiris traveled throughout the world teaching men about agriculture and civilization. When he returned to Egypt, laden with gifts, his grateful people proclaimed him a god.

But, unfortunately, after his travels around the world among cannibalistic savages, Osiris encountered the greatest danger in his own house. His brother, Seth, was jealous of his success and plotted his death with seventy-two friends. For their diabolical scheme, they built a coffin which would just fit Osiris and brought it supposedly as a joke into a feast. Seth offered to give the decorated coffin to the person it would fit, and of course Osiris was the lucky one. When he lay down in the coffin to try it for size, Seth and his friends leaped up and nailed the lid on, soldered it with molten lead, and threw it into the Nile.

Isis fled to the swamps to mourn her husband and to give birth to a son, Horus. In the meantime, the coffin containing Osiris' body floated down the Nile into the Mediterranean and finally drifted ashore in Syria. Trees apparently grow very quickly in that land, because by the time Isis could follow the coffin across the sea, a tree had grown up around it, had been cut down, and made into the pillar of the house of the king of Syria.

When Isis appeared, she served for a time as a nurse for the king's children. At night, she put the baby into the fire to make him immortal while she, in the form of a swallow, fluttered around the pillar containing Osiris' body. But the queen discovered her and screamed in fright, so her child did not become immortal, and Isis was forced to reveal herself. The kind king and queen immediately granted her request for the coffin, and she returned to Egypt.

But after all of her struggles, Isis left the coffin to go visit her son, Horus. In the short time she was gone, Seth found the coffin and, worried that Isis might find some way of resurrecting the body, he cut it up into fourteen pieces and carried each piece to the farthest parts of the kingdom.

Isis again began her search and one by one recovered all of the parts of the body except the genitals, which she replaced with gold. In each place where she found a part of the body, she gave the priests an image of Osiris which was buried and worshipped as his body. Finally she collected all of the parts of the body, which would seem to be a rather useless feat.

But not in ancient Egypt. Ra, the sun god, took pity on Isis' devotion and sent Anubis, the jackal-headed god, to her with a new art—the art of *mummification*. With his secret skills, Anubis pieced together the body of Osiris and made him into a mummy. After Anubis performed all of the proper rites, Osiris came back to life, but in the underworld where he became king.

In Osiris' resurrection, the Egyptians saw their own possibilities for eternal life, for they too could perform the rites of Anubis over their dead. At first only the pharaohs were allowed to become mummies and therefore inherit eternal life, but as time went on, the rites were extended to anyone who could afford them.

As for man, his days are as grass:
As a flower of the field, so he flourisheth.
For the wind passeth over it, and it is gone;
And the place thereof shall know it no more.

PSALM 103:15-16

DEATH AND NATURE

Primitive myths seem to be obsessed with the cycles of nature—the movements of the moon, the rising and setting of the sun, the yearly birth and death of the corn, and the cycle of the seasons. And rightly so, for man's whole life depended on the continuation of these cycles. Many of his ceremonies and the myths they perpetuate are attempts to make sure these cycles will continue. Celebrating the death and rebirth of the corn god ensures that the corn itself will sprout again in spring.

If plants could die each year and rise again, then is it not possible that man, too, could die and rise again? In many cultures, the myths of a dying and rising god of vegetation are closely associated with a belief in eternal life. In worshipping a dying and rising god of the grain, such as Dionysus, Osiris, or Balder, people reaffirmed their hopes for a life beyond death.

the dance of siva

HINDU

Hindu mythology carries the idea of the cycles of life even further than the Greeks and Egyptians. The individual soul dies and then is reincarnated in a new body. In each new life the soul evolves toward understanding until eventually it achieves a state of perfect understanding and is ready to leave the physical world permanently and become united with God.

Furthermore, the universe itself goes through continual cycles of destruction and rebirth. Hindu mythology pictures God as manifested in three forms: Brahma, who creates the world; Vishnu, who preserves it; and Siva, who destroys it when the fullness of time has come.

Siva is also the god of the dance, and his dancing represents the rhythm of the universe. At the end of each age, he dances the Tandava dance which destroys the illusory world of physical existence and causes it to be reintegrated into the world spirit where it waits to be reborn through Brahma.

I have found that life persists in the midst of destruction and, therefore, there must be a higher law than that of destruction.

MAHATMA GANDHI

While supported most strongly in Hindu mythology, the idea of reincarnation has captured men's imaginations in many cultures and ages. On November 29, 1952, in Pueblo, Colorado, an event occurred that made reincarnation a topic of debate all over the United States.

On that night, Morey Bernstein hypnotized a Pueblo housewife and began asking her to remember her childhood. But then he went further.

He asked her to go back to another time and place and to tell him where she was. After waiting a while he asked if a scene from a previous existence had come to her.

The woman answered, breathing heavily. She remembered scratching paint off her bed in anger at getting a spanking.

"What is your name?" the hypnotist asked her.

At first the name sounded like "Friday," but later was corrected to Bridey, Bridey Murphy.

In this session and others, the housewife told in detail about her life as Bridey Murphy in Ireland in 1806. Her father had been a barrister—though Bridey admitted he did some "cropping" or farming. They lived in a nice white house and her room was on the left at the top of the stairs.

As the interview continued, an Irish brogue crept into the Colorado housewife's voice, and soon she began using Irish words and phrases that were very unlikely to have been in a modern American woman's vocabulary.

As the story went on, Bridey told of attending Mrs. Strayne's school in Cork where she learned to be a lady. She married Brian McCarthy, a young lawyer, which caused a certain amount of

335

conflict because she was a Protestant and he was a Catholic. They had no children and apparently lived a rather uneventful life.

Under Bernstein's persistent questioning, Bridey contributed the details of her death: "I fell down stairs . . . it was a terrible burden. I was sixty-six . . . such a burden . . . I had to be carried about."

Then she told of dying, of lingering behind and trying to communicate with her husband, but he wouldn't listen to her. She watched her own funeral and described her tombstone in detail.

She couldn't contribute much about life in the spirit world, except that "you couldn't communicate with anyone very long . . . they'd go away." She was so pleased, though, to discover that there was no purgatory that she waited for Father John, her husband's friend, to die so she could get him to admit he had been wrong.

It was a very interesting story—but could it possibly have been true—and if so, were there records to prove it? Bernstein began to try to elicit details from Bridey's memory that could be checked. Bridey obliged by singing songs she remembered, telling folk tales of her childhood, and describing in detail the town surroundings. She also suggested that her birth, death, and marriage had probably been recorded and suggested that there might have been some articles about her husband in the *Belfast Newsletter.* She also said that Brian had taught at Queens University in Belfast, and there might be some records of him there.

In 1954, the *Denver Post* published three articles about the interviews, and Bernstein then began work on a book, *The Search for Bridey*

Murphy. As part of the research for the book, a reporter was sent to Ireland to try to determine if there really had been a Bridey Murphy. The results of his extensive searches were inconclusive. Little-known details of geography, customs, and language that Bridey had recalled were generally authenticated. But no trace could be found of Bridey Murphy or any of the individuals she mentioned, except perhaps her father-in-law who had a rather common name.

The publication of *The Search for Bridey Murphy* set off considerable controversy. Interest in reincarnation surged, and a number of hypnotists tried to duplicate the experiment. Equally zealous were the disbelievers who tried to find evidence of fraud in the story. Their results were as inconclusive as the search of Irish records. No evidence could be found of any deliberate fraud. The interviews had all been recorded in the presence of witnesses who testified to the integrity of both Bernstein and his subject. Detractors searched movie plots, novels, and the Colorado housewife's own past, but could find no definite source for Bridey's story and knowledge of Ireland. Is the case of Bridey Murphy an example of remembered reincarnation or a freak psychic phenomenon? We will probably never know.

nine hells

In contrast to a belief in reincarnation, many cultures believe there is a special land or lands for the dead. The Aztecs believed there were many places for the dead, and that where a person went depended on how he died.

In the East was the paradise of the sun, where the souls of warriors who fell in combat or died victims of sacrifice went. The southern paradise of Tlaloc was for those who died by drowning, lightning, or leprosy. The western paradise was the house of corn where women who died in childbirth went.

Everyone else had to go through the nine hells to reach a place of eternal peace. First, the dead must cross a deep river A tawny-haired dog was buried with the dead to help him. In the second realm, one had to pass

between two mountains. In the third, the soul had to climb over a mountain of obsidian. In the fourth hell, there was an icy wind. In the fifth hell was a place where flags waved. In the sixth hell, the soul was pierced by arrows. In the seventh hell was a beast that ate human hearts. In the eighth, there was a narrow path between stones. In the ninth hell, the soul found eternal rest.

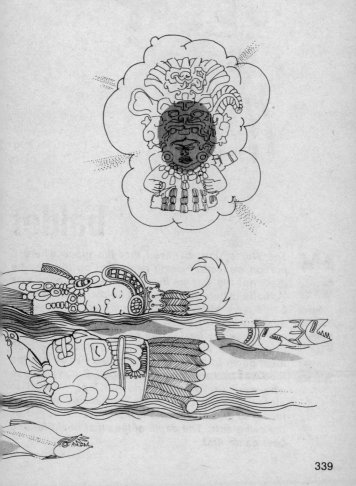

balder

The Norse, too, believed that the place where a person went after death depended on the way he died, not the way he lived. The place of bliss was Valhalla, where only the best soldiers who died in battle were allowed. After each war, the Valkyrie, nine warlike maidens, galloped over the rainbow and chose the best of the dead to go to the home of the gods. The rest were left to Hela, who took them down to a dreary place called Hel, where the food was bad and the company dull. But even those who went to Valhalla could not look forward to eternal bliss, for the gods themselves were not immortal and would eventually all be destroyed by the evil giants. The death of the most beautiful and best came first.

Balder the Beautiful was the best loved and most beautiful of the Norse gods, but he was troubled by dreams warning that he was soon to die. Distressed and troubled, he told his dreams to the other gods. Frigga, his mother, was so upset that she went around the world begging every tree, animal, bird, stone, disease, and poison to promise not to hurt Balder. Since Balder was so well loved by everything all were quite willing to promise.

The other gods were so pleased by Frigga's success that they began to amuse themselves by throwing stones and spears at Balder and watching them all turn aside harmlessly. But Loki the mischief maker delighted in bringing evil upon the gods, and he watched in growing anger as Balder seemed to be safe from harm. Finally he assumed the shape of an old woman and went to visit Frigga.

"Why are all of the other gods throwing things at Balder?" the old woman asked Frigga innocently.

"They are proving the success of the pledges that I have taken from all things on the earth not to hurt Balder," replied Frigga.

"How wonderful," said Loki cunningly. "And did you get this pledge from every single thing on the earth?"

"I did," replied Frigga proudly. "Well, everything except a tiny little shrub called mistletoe that I thought was too young to take an oath."

That was what Loki wanted to know, and he was off immediately to find mistletoe. He picked a twig and rushed back to where the gods were throwing things at Balder.

A little distance off from the others, he found Hoder, who was blind.

"Why aren't you throwing at Balder?" Loki asked in his most friendly voice.

"You know perfectly well that I am blind and can't see where he is," replied Hoder. "And besides, I have nothing to throw."

"Here," said Loki, "throw this twig. I will guide your arm."

So Hoder took the mistletoe, and, guided by Loki, threw it at Balder. The mistletoe pierced Balder's breast and he fell dead in a pool of blood.

The lamentations that went up from the gods have never been equalled since. But Hoder was most unhappy of all. He went to the house of Frigga to ask if there were any way he could take Balder's place.

"No," she replied. "That is impossible. But if someone could ride to Hel, the land of the dead, and ask Hela herself, she might let Balder return."

So Hoder persuaded Hermod, the swiftest of the gods, to go to Hel. For nine days and nights Hermod rode until he came to the bridge over the river Gyoll. He continued until he came to the barred gates of Hel. They were locked, and, seeing no way of opening them, he touched his spurs to his horse and leaped over them.

Hermod pleaded so convincingly that Hela agreed to give him a chance to restore Balder to life.

"If you are telling the truth," she said, "and everything on earth and in Valhalla wants Balder back as badly as you say, I will let him go. If everything in the world, both living and not living, will weep for Balder, then I will let him go."

Hermod hurried back, joyfully, certain that nothing on earth would dare refuse to weep for Balder. The gods immediately sent messengers throughout the world and soon the sound of mourning was heard throughout the world.

However, there was one who would not weep. Loki again assumed the form of an old woman, and when Hermod came begging him to weep, he laughed in his face.

So began the death of the gods which will only end in the final destruction of all Valhalla.

But there is still some hope, for some myths predict that after the destruction of Valhalla and this present earth, Balder will return to rule over a new and better world which will emerge out of the ocean, and during his reign there will be beauty, justice, and happiness.

Part of the fear of death is the fear of the unknown. If only one man could return from the dead and tell us what he found, we could rest more easily. To many ancient Greeks, Orpheus was that man. For Orpheus went to the land of the dead and lived to return. A cult called the Orphic mysteries, which taught its initiates the secrets of death, grew up around his myth.

orpheus

GREEK

Orpheus was the son of the muse Calliope. With this heritage, it is not surprising that he was the most wonderful musician the world has ever known. Not only people but even wild beasts, rocks, and trees loved the music of his lyre.

He fell in love with a girl named Eurydice and of course she could not resist his spell. But their happiness together was short-lived. Shortly after the wedding, a shepherd fell in love with Eurydice and attacked her. As she was fleeing, a serpent bit her and she died.

Overcome with grief, Orpheus resolved to follow her to the land of the dead. Even there, all were charmed into silence by his music. The three-headed dragon-tailed dog Cerberus, who guarded the gates to the underworld, was so charmed by the music that he let Orpheus pass unchallenged. The "shades" of the dead stood in wonder as Orpheus passed before them until he came to Hades and Persephone.

There he sang of his love for Eurydice in such touching strains that even the Furies wept and Hades himself was moved. Under the spell of the music even Hades could not refuse Orpheus' request.

344

Eurydice was brought to him and he was told that she could come back to earth if he would walk the whole distance without looking back at her until they were both out of the underworld. All of Hades held its breath as Orpheus led Eurydice back through all of the horrors of hell. At last he stepped out into the light of the upper world and turned joyfully to her.

Unfortunately, Eurydice was still in the shadows of the underworld, and as soon as his eyes turned upon her, she faded back into the underworld. This time she was lost forever.

For years Orpheus wandered the earth in sorrow until he provoked the wrath of Dionysus and was torn limb from limb by the maenads, Dionysus' followers. Jupiter placed his lyre among the stars, and his spirit returned to the underworld where he finally rejoined Eurydice.

GHOSTS AND SPIRITS

Stories of ghosts, dead spirits that remain in the land of the living, are almost universal—even in cultures that believe in a land of the dead or in reincarnation. Some of these ghosts are friendly and helpful—particularly one's own ancestors if they are worshipped properly. Some are lonely figures looking for their loved ones. But most are beings of terror and horror who punish those who have wronged them and seek to take others with them into death.

348

An African Ghost Tale

Huese and Hueve's mother died when they were born, and they were reared by their stepmother. She treated them badly and made them work hard. One day she sent them to get water in two small gourds, but Huese fell and broke his gourd. Wanting to share his brother's punishment, Hueve broke his too. The stepmother whipped them both cruelly.

Tearfully the two boys decided to go to death's door and try to see their mother. On hearing their story, the guardian of death's door let them pass and they found themselves in two markets—the market of the living and the market of the dead. Then they found their mother.

After hearing their story, she went first to the market of the living and bought them two new gourds. Then she went to the land of the dead and bought some palm nuts which she told the twins to give their stepmother as a present.

When the twins returned, the stepmother laughed at the story, but she eagerly ate the palm nuts, for they were her favorite food. Immediately after eating them, she died. Frightened by her sudden death, the family went to a diviner who spoke to the ghost of the stepmother.

"Tell all of the other wives," she said, "that I died because I mistreated the twins. Tell the other women that when they are given stepchildren or orphans to care for they must love them and treat them as their own so they will not meet the same fate that I did."

A Pawnee Ghost Tale

Long, long ago a group of young men went to visit a neighboring village. While they were gone, the girl friend of one of the men died and the rest of the tribe left the village and went on a hunt. Most of the young men joined their friends on the hunt, but the young man, who did not know that his people had moved and his sweetheart had died, returned to the old village.

When he got near the village, he saw that it was empty, except for his girl friend, who was sitting in front of a lodge.

"What are you doing here alone?" he asked.

"I had a quarrel with my family and they left me here," she replied.

"Well, then, let's get married right now," the young man said.

"No, we must return to our people and wait a little while," she replied.

When they came near the new village, the girl said that it was very important that no one see her and that the young man not tell anyone she was with him.

"Prepare a place for me where I can spend four days and nights behind a curtain," she said.

The young man agreed and went into the village. He fixed up an area of his lodge for the girl and sent one of his female relatives to get her.

"Who is the girl I am to get?" asked his relative, and the young man, forgetting what his sweetheart had told him, spoke her name.

"Why, that girl died several weeks ago," said the startled relative.

Sure enough, when the young man went to look for his sweetheart, she was gone. That night he died in his sleep. If he had not disobeyed her request, she would have come back to life after four days.

HOTTENTOT

In the olden days, the moon sent a message to man that "As I die and dying live, so you shall also die and dying live." She asked an insect to carry the message to mankind for her.

The insect started taking the message, but on the way, the hare caught up with her and asked where she was going. The insect replied that she had a very important message for man.

"You are so slow. Let me take the message," said the hare.

"All right," said the insect.

So the hare ran on to man. But when he arrived, he delivered the message in this way. He said, "The moon has sent this message. When I die, I perish, and when you die, you will also perish altogether."

When the moon found out what the rabbit had done, she hit the rabbit on the nose with a stick. To this day, rabbits have a slit nose, and man believes that when he dies he will perish.

THE GREAT MISTAKE

351

accepting death

There is a story of an old Taoist scholar who lost his dearly beloved wife. His friends and relatives came to mourn with him, but they found him sitting on the floor and beating a drum and singing.

"How can you do this?" his friends demanded. "After all of the years you spent with her, how can you be cheerful at her death?"

"I do love my wife," replied the Taoist. "And when she died I despaired because she was gone. But then I began to think and realized that this is what life is. After all, if I had died first, she would have had to remarry, perhaps someone she did not love, and our children would have been hungry and abused.

"Tears will not change the way life is. My wife is now at peace. If I were to make a lot of noise weeping and wailing, I would disturb her rest. It would show that I know nothing of the ways of life and death."

Stamped
on buttocks:
100 year free lease
must be re-turned

If you're reconciled with death or even if you are pretty well assured that you will have a good death, a dignified one, then every single moment of every single day is transformed because the pervasive undercurrent—the fear of death—is removed. . . . I am living an end-life where everything ought to be an end in itself, where I shouldn't waste any time preparing for the future, or occupying myself with means to later end. . . .

You get stabbed by things, by flowers and by babies and by beautiful things—just the very act of living, of walking and breathing and eating and having friends and chatting. Everything seems to look more beautiful rather than less, and one gets the much-intensified sense of miracles.

ABRAHAM MASLOW

The Buddha once told this parable:

There was once a man who was crossing a field and met a tiger. Running, he came to a great cliff and caught hold of a root and swung over the side of the cliff. But at the bottom of the cliff was another tiger.

Soon two little mice came along and began to gnaw on the vine. The man looked in terror at the tiger below. But then he saw a strawberry vine. He picked the strawberry and ate it. How delicious it was.

MYTHS BY COUNTRY OF ORIGIN

GREEK AND ROMAN

AMERICAN INDIAN AND USA

AFRICA

ORIENT AND MIDDLE EAST

EUROPE

Photo Credits

Abbott Laboratories: page i

Charles Beard: page 16

Denver Art Museum: page 44

Elliott Erwitt, Magnum: page 47

Boston Museum of Fine Arts: page 74

UPI: pages xiii, 123

NASA: page 190

Reprinted from *Garuda*, published by Karma Dzong and Tail of the Tiger Buddhist Communities: pages 225-29

Wide World: page 301

Another Mother for Peace: pages 306-08

Michael Kinnicutt, copyright, ©, 1971, by Blue Mountain Arts: page 309

Barbara Gianulis, Kansas University: page 322

Reprinted from *Square Sun, Square Moon*, by Paul Reps, by permission of the publisher, Charles E. Tuttle, Co., Inc.: page 352

Courtesy of New York Public Library Picture Collection: pages 11, 17, 18, 24, 46-47, 51, 57, 103, 125, 148, 159, 243, 249, 271, 312, 319, 326

All other illustrations by Jay and Sherwood Roper

ABOUT THE AUTHORS

BARBARA STANFORD holds an A.B. in English from the University of Illinois and an M.A. in the teaching of English from Columbia University. For six years she taught English at Vashon High School in St. Louis, Missouri, and is presently a teacher of English at Fairview High School, Boulder, Colorado. Mrs. Stanford is author of *Negro Literature for High School Students* and co-author of *Theory and Practice in the Teaching of Literature by Afro-Americans*, both published by the National Council of Teachers of English. Her other publications include an anthology of black literature and, with her husband, two world literature texts and accompanying composition program. She is a frequent program participant in multi-ethnic literature at the annual convention of the NCTE, and is author of numerous articles in education journals.

GENE STANFORD holds an A.B. in English from Washington University and an M.A. in Guidance and Counseling from the University of Colorado. He taught English for four years at Horton Watkins High School in suburban St. Louis and is presently an NDEA Doctoral Fellow in Education at the University of Colorado. Mr. Stanford is author of a composition text, a vocabulary improvement program, and an anthology on the generation gap. He is co-author, with Mrs. Stanford, of *Learning Discussion Skills Through Games* and, with Albert E. Roark, of *Human Interaction in Education*. His articles appear frequently in education journals.